HALLOWEEN

The Quintessential British Guide
to Treats and Frights

Also by Kristoffer Hughes –
   NATURAL DRUIDRY

HALLOWEEN

The Quintessential British Guide to Treats and Frights

By
Mark Doody and Kristoffer Hughes

THOTH PUBLICATIONS
Loughborough, Leicestershire

Published by Thoth Publications
64, Leopold Street, Loughborough, LE11 5DN

ISBN: 978-1-913660-01-7

web address: www.thoth.co.uk
email: enquiries@ thoth.co.uk

DEDICATION

To the memory of Rachel Anne Davies
You will always be remembered

ACKNOWLEDGEMENTS

Mark & Kris wish to warmly thank the following people for their invaluable input, advice, comments, help, and humour. Sarah and Lauren Doody for their tireless support and being guinea pigs for the food and drinks created for this book, and also for providing copious amounts of Vodka and other brain numbing beverages. Ian Gibbs for all the meals cooked ensuring that malnutrition would not get in the way. A big thank you to Scream Queen for her inimitable assistance and her partner in crime the Pumpkin King! Tara Jade for her friendship, care and support and the loan of her mansion! Michelle for her dedicated internet trawling skills in search of quotes and titbits and her kind observations. Tom Clarke for taking a chance on a crazy book! Thanks also to the delectably gorgeous Philippe Vidal, animator extraordinaire and font of French wisdom. Humble thanks to Peter Stockinger for providing invaluable information on Austrian traditions. Thanks to Tom at Halloweenerrific, a fellow Halloween nut, for his support in publicising this book, keep up the good work. Edward and Douglas from Midnight Syndicate for their kindness, support and amazing music that has kept us in suitable Halloween mood all year round. Finally, thanks also to all our beloved dead, without whom, we wouldn't have a Halloween.

CONTENTS

ANTE - MORTEM

Where there is no imagination – there is no Horror
(Sir Arthur Conan Doyle)

The wheel of the year turns on its axis, the last warm rays of summer have long since passed; leaves sigh and fall from branches, tired and weary after months of display. It is late October, darkness and cold encroaches upon the land, singing it to sleep. As trees slumber and nature rests something peculiar stirs within the imagination of mankind. What may appear as an ordinary late autumn evening is in fact something quite extraordinary. Shadows dance in corners, whispering ghouls float between houses, peels of glee and terror ring through the night. Something wicked this way comes, or so it may seem.

The feast at the end of October invokes an ancient magic that rises from the depth of our ancestry, a calling that connects us to over 2,000 years of history. Yet this history is peculiar for it embodies a quality unlike the majority of annual festivals and celebrations that mankind has adopted. The feast at the end of October is one of mischief, of guising, of ghouls and spirits and things that go bump in the night.

Terror, horror, superstition and suspense fill the heavy dark air, whilst peals of laughter and screams of exaggerated terror ring through villages and towns. Candles blaze in windows, cemeteries glow with eerie lights that flicker in the wind. Spring and summer give way to autumn and just as autumn decrees its surrender to winter, something odd happens and we all feel it, some of us detest it, some dread it, whilst others delight in its contrasting colours and nature.

Something within the bizarre rituals and traditions of October feels familiar, like echoes from past times we sense a remembering, as if memories of times gone by rise up to invoke something within mankind. Accentuated by the vibrant colours of late autumn, cooling nights and flickering lights, by myth and fairytale, the primary feast of October is firmly entrenched in the human psyche. Whatever our involvement, however we choose to express our connection to this feast we can no longer avoid its influence on our year and in our lives.

It is perhaps the oldest of festivals, one that arose from the land of Britain to inspire the world! This is Halloween, the British Feast of the Dead.

The purpose of this book is threefold, primarily its nature is one of reclamation, as the first part of this book will demonstrate, the festival of Halloween is rooted in British heritage not, as many would assume, in American history. Therefore our main drive for compiling this work is the desire to reclaim Halloween as a recognisable British festival. We strive to bring Halloween back home!

Secondly the book will provide an overview of its history and development over countless centuries, and its progression through time to the modern era, we do this not as a historical tome but to provide the reader with an authoritative background into the *"Why's and What for's"* of Halloween. Gaining an understanding of its origins provides a framework for celebration, it educates us to understand why we do it, where it came from and that culturally it is important to maintain the traditions and preserve them for future generations. Its inherent *Britishness* should be something that instils a sense of heritage and cultural pride. The historical section of this book will not only serve to educate and inform but also provide further opportunities to participate in ancient traditions that are worthy of resurrection, we will provide detailed accounts of ancient traditions and how we can practise them today. Incorporating these practises into modern celebration will enhance your current traditions, bringing an older, authentic angle to them. There are plenty of Halloween 'How To Books' currently on the market, but our hope is that this one will differ greatly from the norm by its combination of history, ancient and modern practise and inspiration.

Thirdly, the book will provide you with instructions, inspiration and information in respect to the celebration of Halloween in the 21st century. This is the expressive face of Halloween in its entire scary, tacky, aesthetic and fun-filled guise. The art of celebrating through costume, feasting and decorating is not a new or current invention; it is vital part of the festival. Celebrating connects us to something far older than us, older than the generations that we can recall before us. All the plastic, the black cloth and orange lights, the rubber skeletons and glowing jack-o-lanterns have a purpose, and the sense of enjoyment we get from them carries the magic that is Halloween.

However as with most things in life they have a beginning, they have history, they actually mean something. Gaining an understanding and appreciation of this meaning enhances our experience of feasting and celebrating, it brings it to life, or as in the case of Halloween; it brings the dead back amongst the living. The typical horror themes of Halloween are not simply frivolous expressions inspired by Hollywood, they are; surprisingly rooted in Celtic history, the scaremongering and terrorising of neighbourhoods and children is, as you will find something deeply rooted in our cultural consciousness.

Halloween is this and so much more, it is perhaps the most vibrant and enjoyable of British festivals and this book seeks to reclaim that and more. We don't need to know where it comes from to have a good time and to scare the local kids senseless, but it is there and it is ours so an appreciation of that not only justifies our passion for Halloween but accentuates it. There is very little left of British culture and it may surprise many that Halloween is originally British, it is cultural, however silly and tacky it may seem it hides a deeper, older magic. This book arose from that connection.

But how does this happen? Two grown men from different parts of the country with contrasting lifestyles come together for the love of one thing, for the fun-fuelled, ghost driven, spookiness of a single night in October! Traumatised by childhood nightmares of Swedes and bin bags, these two men form an unlikely partnership in pursuit of a single goal...to make Halloween as monumental an event as is practised by our cousins across the pond in the United States of America. The Americans do it so well, but so can we; after all it was ours to begin with.

So, we invite you on a journey with two guys who live for the 31st of October, who chuckle in delight as supermarkets fill their shelves with imported plastic tat. Who squeal in glee at the horrified cries of guests terrorised by scenes of horror and pretence. Men who also acknowledge the sombreness of the season in its reverential form but also collapses (well one of them does) to his knees and screams like a girl when met with an actor in a mask! So, wait until dusk, put the kettle on and settle on the sofa and take a ride with two, somewhat unhinged guys who just know how to do Halloween so well!

Mark Doody & Kristoffer Hughes,
Isle of Anglesey & Sutton Coldfield,
April 2011

PART 1

DIGGING UP THE DEAD
The Origins of Halloween

When the world is wrapped in slumber
And the moon is sailing high,
If you peep between the curtains,
You'll catch spirits riding by.
(Early 20th century Halloween postcard)

This section will provide you with a historical overview of the festival of Halloween, where it came from, why it developed and how it was practised over the last several hundreds of years. Eventually we will reach the modern era and the current face of Halloween, by the time we get to this bit you will know quite a bit about this festival that should bemuse your friends, and stand you on good ground in any pub quiz!

The seemingly innocent practises and traditions that surround Halloween may appear sacrilegious to some and yet entirely harmless to others. Some folk consider them quaint, something that children partake of, and that's it, end of story, pointless and childlike. The reality is quite the contrary, for behind the apparent innocence and costumes, beneath the incessant cries of "Trick or Treat" hide sacred ceremonies whose roots reach back, through the mists of time to the dawning of civilisation.

When darkness falls and an inevitable knocking is heard upon the door. When ghouls and ghosts; stand with hands beseeching offerings of chocolate and sweets. When a neighbour's house displays a large hollowed pumpkin, whose flesh is carved in ghastly guise and flickers with internal light, warns that this is no ordinary night. The ghouls at your door present a warning, a treat or a trick? They embody the spirit of mischief and rebuke them at your peril, for the disguise belies an ancient practise older than the standing stones that decorate the countryside. Our fun-filled Halloween is far older than you may imagine, it is a festival of contradiction, a perfect blending of Pagan and Christian traditions and beliefs.

Every tale, every story, everything has a beginning, a point in time, where something came into existence. To find the first stirrings of Halloween, we must travel back in time to around 2,500 years ago when the Iron Age Celts occupied the islands of Britain and most of northern Europe. It is more than likely that the feast known today as Halloween is much older than this, but generally this is a good place to start exploring its history; everything prior to this date gets a little murky. Stuff wasn't written down much at this point in time, but we know enough about the Iron Age Celts to begin here.

Although the Etymology or the origin of the word Halloween is Christian, its traditional associations are far from Christian and belong to the distant Pagan past of the British Isles and northern France. To the Celts of the Iron Age the period we now call Halloween was known as *"Samhain"* pronounced *"Sow-en"*, the word is derived from the Celtic Gaelic language and is of some antiquity. Roughly translated the word *Samhain* means *"summer's end"*. It marked the end of a season and the transition into another, a time when folk would gather to celebrate, a tradition which continues to this day. Contrary to some internet sources, *Samhain* was not a Druidic god of death.

The Celts lived very different lives from our own, unlike our modern lives theirs were entirely dependent on nature to survive. If the crops failed or the harvest was meagre it meant certain death to the poor, the weak and the elderly. If fodder was inadequate, the animals would in turn suffer and not survive the long winter months ahead. We are able to drive or walk to the nearest super-market and purchase anything we wish regardless of the season, our ancestors could not. Consequently festivals like Halloween are steeped with ancestral memory from a time when life was difficult, tough, when the attainment of food was something real and something that could go terribly wrong. But, we can assume that most years the preparations were good and nature rewarded the hard work of the people. The feast of *Samhain* celebrated not only the fully stocked larders, but also took into account those who were no longer present.

A continuous theme can be observed throughout the Pagan, Christian and ordinary world, it is that of the dead. Although the *Samhain*/Halloween celebrations do not in any shape or form revere death itself, it is focussed instead on those who have passed beyond the veil and into the world beyond. However, the Celts believed that on the eve of *Samhain* the veils or the doors between our world and the world of the dead was thin, and would not hold fast the dead and thus allow them entry into our world. Now this could be a blessing or a curse, depending who the dead were, a departed parent or sibling would be welcomed back amidst the living, but a rival chieftain or evildoer would not.

Supernatural forces and the powers of dying and decay were most prevalent during this time, and the Celts genuinely believed that the spirits of the dead wandered amongst the living. But where does all this come from? One probable explanation is that *Samhain,* just like our modern Halloween was and is a "*Liminal*" time. Liminality is a word used to describe something that is betwixt and between. We continue to this day to be affected by liminal time and space, whether we are conscious of it or not. Liminality can be defined in relation to time as the point just before dawn, or the period of dusk where it is neither light nor dark. Midnight and noon are liminal points on the clock, they stand between times. In the cycle of the seasons liminality is the point at which a season moves from one to another. *Samhain* is one example. For those who understand Astrology we are exactly at 15 degrees of Scorpio, we stand at the threshold between autumn and winter, neither in one nor the other but somewhere between. The trees are almost asleep, the natural world is yawning and preparing for slumber, the world feels tired. Undeniably the darkness reigns supreme, and somehow it can be felt to laugh and snigger at the weakening light of the sun, who's brightness is barely enough to keep us going through the working day.

It is generally spooky at this time of year, so no great surprise that the ancient Celts celebrated a festival that acknowledged supernatural powers; honoured the dead and celebrated the reorganising of communities and the bounty of the harvest. The feast of *Samhain* akin to the other 3 major Celtic festivals of *Imbolc* (spring), *Beltane* (summer) and *Lughnassadh* (first harvest) was known as a "Fire Festival", and it is believed that the Celts built enormous bonfires to ward off malevolent spirits and unwanted attention from the dead. It is no coincidence that another major British festival remains to this day and continues the theme of bonfires. Guy Fawkes Night or Bonfire night, referring to the gunpowder plot, retains elements of the ancient *Samhain* practises of lighting fires to ward off spirits and to provide warmth and hope at the beginning of winter. Today, Guy Fawkes Night has lost most of its historical meaning in the general popular mind, but hidden within it are references and rituals far older than the gunpowder plot itself.

Although we do not know what exactly happened at the *Samhain* festivities as the Celts rarely wrote anything down, we do know that it was important to them and is noted in several calendars, the ancient Coligny calendar being one of them. Written on a bronze tablet during the early half of the second century, it states that the festival of *Samhain* was celebrated over a period of three nights known as *"Trinoxtion Samonii"* or the three nights of *Samhain*. I for one, take this as ample evidence for the justification of a 3 night long celebration of Halloween; as if I even need to justify it!

An interesting fact here is that time is not seen to be measured by days but rather by nights, a general delineation of time during the era of the Celts. Surprisingly we continue to use this system, albeit somewhat subconsciously, by using terms such as *"Fortnight"* to describe two weeks, quantified by nights not by days. Interestingly the term Fortnight is not generally used anywhere other than within the islands of Britain, another link to our Celtic ancestry.

The supernatural qualities of Halloween have been preserved to this day, and no Halloween would be complete without the requisite screams and all things that go bump in the night. Even as *Samhain* morphed and transformed over the centuries, eventually to be incorporated into the Christian tradition, it maintained its link with the supernatural world. Thanks to the Church the festival was inadvertently preserved forever.

During the 7th century Pope Boniface IV dedicated the Pantheon, a Roman temple which he consecrated as a church to the Virgin Mary and all martyrs; those who had died in service of their faith. Their feast day was the 13th of May. This day was to become known as *All Saints Day* which was eventually moved in the 8th century by another Pope called Gregory III to November the 1st, because those pesky Pagan's couldn't have the festival all to themselves now could they! So in a similar theme to the feast of *Samhain,* the eve of which was celebrated on the 31st of October and the 1st of November was known as Samhain Day, it suddenly became popularly known as *All Hallows Eve*, Hallow being an old English word for Saint; the night before All Saints Day. The church threw in another feast on the 2nd of November called *All Souls Day* when people would pray for the souls of those held in purgatory.

The Christian tradition celebrated God and the saints, exemplary individuals who gave up their lives to the church during the feast of All Saints, oddly mimicking the ancient practises of the Celtic *Samhain*. Nothing is entirely original, throughout time traditions and mythologies have been borrowed, stolen and adopted by incoming traditions and religions.

The period of All Hallows also had a practical aspect to it which echoes the previous Pagan traditions, it was the time of slaughter; and in medieval Britain the annual slaughter traditionally took place at Hallowmas or Hallowtide. It was only a matter of time, and the natural evolution of language that All Hallows Eve turned into Hallowmas, All Hallows and eventually Hallowe'en. The only difference today is the little apostrophe is commonly removed giving us the familiar Halloween. In Wales the eve of Halloween is known as *Nos Calan Gaeaf* or the eve of the calends of winter, also known in medieval times as *Ysbrydnos;* spirit night. As you can see the theme of the dead and all that is creepy continues in current Celtic language to demonstrate the power Halloween has had, not simply on our imaginations but also on our language.

The turning point in the celebration of Halloween happened during the middle ages, as thankfully, folk started writing stuff down, documenting local traditions and events. This is when the traditions, rituals and practises of Halloween as we know them today started in earnest and snowballed into the 20th century mass market celebrations that have continued to this day. Remarkably nearly every practise that you may be familiar with has an older more ancient predecessor, everything that we do in fact is inspired from the deep, dark past.

The modern face of Halloween is dominated by three distinct groups, two of which work well side by side, whilst the other is somewhat opposing. Firstly we have the celebrants, those who just love the plastic and tat, the partying and dressing up, those who throw themselves into the festivities with vigour and passion. Houses get dressed up, lights flicker, decorations and props serve to scare the living daylights out of guests and passersby. The second group are the Neo-Pagans, who see an element of sacredness to the proceedings and celebrate it, not dissimilar to the first group, but with the added spiritual element thrown in for good measure. Modern Pagans seek to reclaim the sacred ceremonies and traditions of Halloween in a manner which is simultaneously reverent and frivolous. It is the perfect blend of the sublime and the profane. The third demographic are the fundamental Christian groups who serve to demonise the festival as "Evil" or even satanic. They have encouraged schools and other establishments to ban Halloween decorations and events, publically denouncing the festival as un-Christian. However, this group serves only to demonstrate the ignorance of its own tradition and its influence on the festival, and that a Christian feast of the dead is permanently embedded in the festival of Halloween.[1]

---

1. Hutton, Ronald Professor: *Stations of the Sun.*

TRADITIONS AND SYMBOLS

So, there we have it a concise history of how Halloween came about, but of course no history would be complete without a brief examination of the traditions and practises that arose from the deep, dark past, many of which continue to this day. Similar to the Christmas festival, Halloween is riddled with defined symbolism which leave no doubt in the observers mind that what he or she is seeing is something to do with Halloween. Whether these items be Jack O Lanterns, ghosts and witches, hanging skulls, black ravens or a cauldron full of apples, they define the season by means of symbols, and symbology is a powerful thing, far more powerful than folk give it credit. Symbology allows us to identify and understand something by representing its nature to us in a creative, expressive manner. We don't need to understand the symbols for them to be effective, in a way that is not their point. Their intent is to instil a sense of understanding in the observer (handy if you are advertising a product or selling a movie) so that what they see is without a doubt recognisably Halloween. Without the use of symbols none of our festivals, events, clubs, organisations and politicians; to name but a few, would be effective. With the use of symbology something can become firmly embedded in the popular consciousness, it begins a life of its own, fed by those who identify with it. This fact is firmly found and easily demonstrated in the rites of Halloween. But everything starts somewhere.

Pumpkin Madness

Perhaps the Jack O Lantern or carved pumpkin is the primary identifiable symbol of Halloween in the late 20th and early 21st centuries. Its history is as colourful as Halloween itself. In centuries past the traditional illumination used by guisers and mummers during the festive season were varied selections of root vegetables, ranging from Swede's, turnips and mangel wurzels. These were found in most regions of the United Kingdom during the last few hundred years or so, and were particularly well established traditions in some of England's south western counties. These vegetables were hollowed out and then carved with hideous features to represent spirits and goblins. Commonly, long before the term Jack O Lantern was adopted these lanterns were referred to as "Spunkie's" or "Punkie's". Interestingly the term "Spunkie" also refers to ignited marsh gas also known as Will-o-the-Wisp. The tradition of "Punkie's" would see children wander from door to door in their locality whilst singing:

> *"It's Punkie night, its punkie night,*
> *Give us a candle, give us a light,*
> *If 'ee don't, we'll give 'ee a fright."*

The aim of the game was to receive some form of treat from the residents who would otherwise risk a trick being played upon them instead. Although many claim that the link from this tradition to the modern Trick-or-Treat tradition is tenuous, it is easy to imagine how this and other old practises got thrown into a huge cauldron; stirred around a bit and arose as the popular Trick-or-Treat practises of today. It all started with a humble vegetable! However the vegetable lanterns had a common theme that still prevails to this day and must, logically, hearken back to Pagan times; that the lanterns all represent aspects of death and spirits, and in some parts of the United Kingdom they were symbols of the dead. The tradition of the root vegetable being given the title Jack O Lantern comes from an old Irish legend about a peculiar guy called Stingy Jack.

According to the story, several centuries ago in the west of Ireland, there lived an old drunkard called "Jack the Smith". Jack was known throughout the land as a deceiver, liar, manipulator and an altogether unpleasant type of man. One fateful night, the devil is said to have overheard the tale of Jack's evil deeds and vicious tongue. Intrigued by such claims and slightly envious, it is said that the devil went to meet old Jack to find out for himself if the rumours about him were true.

Typically, old Jack was drunk and stumbling home from the local tavern when he happened across a corpse in the road.

Jack, aware that he was the first to see the corpse, smiled to himself at the thought of stealing its possessions, alas for jack, the corpse was in fact the devil in disguise. Jack assumed that this would be the end of him and that the devil had finally come to take his soul down to the pits of hell. However this was not a man who gave up so easily and so Jack made a last request: He asked that the devil allow him one final drink before taking his soul.

The devil did not object to the request and took Jack to the nearest tavern and supplied him with the finest ale. Much to his surprise, upon quenching his thirst, Jack asked the devil to pay the tab on the ale. Jack then convinced the devil, who had no money upon his person to transform into a silver coin by which to pay the bartender. Impressed by Jack's sheer cheek, the devil agreed, and turned himself into a silver coin. Shrewdly, Jack stuck the now transformed devil into his pocket, which just happened to contain a silver cross. The cross's presence prevented the devil from escaping his form. This coerced the devil to agree to Jack's demand: in exchange for the devil's freedom, the devil promised to spare Jack's soul for the next year. Chuckling to himself, Jack went on his way and merrily had the best year of his life knowing that he had shamed the devil.

A year later to the date when Jack originally struck his deal, he found history to repeat itself, and once again took audience with the devil. On a moonlit night he happened across the devil grinning menacingly beneath a tree on a country lane. "Pray do not take an old man's soul without allowing him some food." pleaded Jack. The devil bemused, agreed to Jack's request to climb the apple tree next to him and fetch him a ripe fruit for his last supper. The devil agreed and climbed the tree, upon returning he found that he could not leave the branches of the tree, and discovered to his dismay that Jack had carved a cross upon the trunk of the tree. Bewildered the devil agreed to Jack's next request, to allow him 10 years free of pursuit, and to promise that he would not take Jack's soul to hell upon his death. The devil, with a malevolent chuckle, agreed.

Eventually Jack's life of living in the fast lane and the consumption of too much alcohol took its toll and Jack died. As his soul prepared to enter the gates of heaven he was met by St. Peter who denied him access to the realms beyond on account of his deceit and drinking. Dejected Jack took himself to the gates of hell where he was met by the devil, he begged for admission into the underworld. However, the devil adhering to his own promise informed Jack that he could not possibly break his promise and take his soul into hell. The devil took a little pity on Jack, for he secretly admired him, and gave him an eternally glowing ember from the fire-pits of hell. Jack was then cursed to walk between the worlds, neither in heaven nor hell, with his glowing ember inside a hollowed turnip to give him some light and warmth.

To this day and until the end of time, Jack is doomed to roam the between-world. But on certain days when the veils are thin, the grotesque face carved on his turnip can be seen glowing bright in the darkness to the sounds of Jack's cries for mercy and forgiveness. From that day to this the deceitful old man was known as Jack of the lantern.

No one is entirely sure how old this tale is, but the chances are it existed in various forms for a number of centuries in Ireland, and may well have existed in another form in the earlier narrative traditions before the arrival of the church. However, the story had significant impact on the Celtic population of Ireland and the *Samhain*/Halloween festivities were centralised around hollowed out vegetables. They would glow in windows mimicking the light from jack's lantern. With the mass immigration of the Irish to the United States of America the indigenous Pumpkin was introduced to them, and with its large cavity and easily removable flesh it soon became the lantern of choice. Its colour mimicking the bright orange and reds of the fall leaves, its carved features a warning to other spirits to stay away, its light mimicking the eternal suffering of poor Jack lost in the between-world.

So, although a Pumpkin is pretty, looks good and celebrates the season, as you can see it also represents something ancient and indigenously Celtic in nature. Its sings of the origin of the festival that arises from the mists of time, changing as it does with each decade with each new society that adopts its symbology. Perhaps that is the beauty of Halloween; it continuously evolves thus ensuring its own survival by sheer persistence and perpetuation.

The Pumpkin has developed newer more appropriate symbology in the last two decades, one being that it acts as an open display to the receptiveness of residents to visitations from ghouls and goblins in disguise who come knocking for treats. It has also been incorporated into the festivals association with the dead, and the pumpkin light is said to shine from windows to guide the spirits of the dead to share an evening of celebration and remembrance with their living descendents. Another explanation for the use of the Jack O Lantern is that they represent the Christian concept of lost souls in purgatory, and that the lights serve to guide them to paradise.

According to Professor Nicholas Rogers; Halloween and its pumpkins are now shamelessly secular without any explicit reference to souls in purgatory with which they may have originally been associated. Although Jack O Lanterns may commemorate the wandering of souls hardly anyone acknowledges or understands this historical reference.[2] Nowadays the carved pumpkin represents the bizarre, the macabre the weird and the scary and it does so without apology. Recently, and mostly due to the influence of Hollywood and perhaps a smattering of Celtic association, the pumpkin is regarded as a protective device; an object which repels any malevolent spirits and defends the home and its residents from the unfriendly spirits that may be walking abroad. Regardless of its associations the pumpkin is without doubt the King of Halloween symbology.

---

2. Rogers, Nicholas: *Halloween, from Pagan ritual to party night*, p164-165.

Apple Bobbery!

...and danglery! No Halloween would be complete without the humble apple, whether they are hung from a string or bobbing about in a vat of water. Who knew that apples could be such fun, even if the living room may resemble a scene from the 'Poseidon Adventure' a jolly good time will have been had by all. And there is nothing better to put a grimace on a mothers face than a cold vat of murky water stained with makeup and spit on the 1st of November! Just like our pumpkins the Apple also belies a history steeped in magic and sacred ceremony.

The apple is perhaps one of the last fruits to be collected before the approaching winter; to our ancestors the apple would have been a nourishing and sweet staple during the cold months. It was believed by the Celts of Ireland and Wales that the fairies would spit upon fruit that remained on branches after the 31st of October making them quite inedible. We may never truly know the origin of the apples association with Halloween, but little snippets of information have slipped through the mesh of time. The Celts apparently believed that the apple was a symbol of the divine feminine and fertility, indeed if cut in half the apple's seed-core resembles the five pointed star or pentacle; a sacred symbol of nature used by many traditions throughout time. The apple also has close associations with a roman Goddess called 'Pomona', the goddess of fruits, in particular the apple. Many believe that the Romans introduction of their goddess harmoniously merged with indigenous Celtic beliefs in the sacredness of apples, and morphed over time from deific attributions to the party delights of today.

The apple has long been identified in worldwide mythology as a fruit of knowledge and mystery, from the fateful apple in the Garden of Eden to German Norse paganism to the Halloween custom of bobbing. The apple ignites the imagination. Even as kids, I have happy memories of 'scrumping', the stealing of apples from someone's tree, naughty yes, but good fun nonetheless. The practice of apple bobbing was originally a form of divination; it was said that a girl could foresee her future husband by peeling and apple on All Hallows Eve in front of a mirror, and discern the letter of his name from peelings when cast onto the floor. Over the centuries it has lost its divinatory aspect and morphed into a party game.

The concept of Apple Bobbing or ducking as they call it in Scotland is now firmly embedded in the practice of Halloween. Snap apple is also a popular British based game, where apples are hung on string and the players must consume them with their hands tied behind their backs. Try doing it with a sugared donut, where the licking of lips is forbidden!

Mischief Making – Guising, Tricking and Treating

The actual origin of Trick or Treating is somewhat lost to us, there is no doubt that the tradition itself is steeped in history and probably conveys aspects of ancient ceremonies. However within this rather peculiar practise hides magic, mystery and bizarre ritual. We can more or less be sure that the ancient Celts did not practise Trick or Treating, but some of the old traditions of the Celts are responsible for inspiring the modern Trick or Treat. But of course the actual act of Treat or Treating has a rule, an unspoken one perhaps, but none the less it is there; you *must* be in disguise. In my own personal Halloween tradition it is a rule that if a Trick or Treater arrives and is not in guise then no treats are bestowed upon them, after all the intent is to be hidden behind a veil of mischief and spookiness. But why dress up, and why the near begging for sweets?

What can be surmised about the festival is that over the centuries, throughout the Pagan Celtic and Christian era of its existence, it has long been established as a night of mischief. The reason for this is simple, from the liminal time of *Samhain*, to the ancestral, spirit associations of All Saints and All souls day, normal social rules are suspended, in particular on the eve of Samhain or All Hallows Day. For reasons locked into our social subconscious the eve of Halloween is a time when the world is turned on its end, anything is possible, nothing is truly impossible; we can become someone else for the night, act differently than normal. Permission to scare and to be scared is almost mandatory, expected, yet generally we don't know why we do it or why we seemingly enjoy it so much. The fact that we do enjoy it sings of its value, the manner and vigour by which we throw ourselves into it expresses a connection to the macabre and the bizarre that is totally anathema to our behaviour during the rest of the year.

There are several possible roots for the traditions of guising and tricking, all of them exclusively arise from the Islands of Britain, nullifying any argument that Halloween is an American created holiday. First and foremost it arises from the general association the festival has with ghosts, witches, spirits and goblins. It was believed that not all spirits were of good intent, and superstition held that some spirits may whisk you away to the between-worlds for reasons known only to them. The most effective method to deceive the spirits was to mimic them, a mask or cowl or hood would disguise the face and perhaps cause the spirit to believe that you too were not mortal. People of most civilisations throughout history have traditionally given offerings to the ancestors or the dead, so it is no great leap of the imagination to recognise that the ghoul which appears on your doorstep on the 31st of October actually is an ancient tradition of mimicking the dead. The sweets you handover may well be offerings of pacification, withhold a treat and they may wreck havoc, oddly reflecting the threat that the spirits may kidnap you or cause you some trouble.

As time went by, many traditions evolved to serve the spirit of Halloween. In the north western part of Wales there was an odd practise which involved a tailless black sow who lay in wait for unsuspecting children that may be out at night. Men would pretend to be the great sow and begin their chase in local cemeteries, the children would respond by knocking on doors and asking for food to cast onto the ground to hopefully slow the sow's relentless chase. It's easy to see how that practise alone could have inspired modern Trick or Treating. But, perhaps more convincingly is the medieval ritual called "Souling" which involved a door to door procession and the singing of a traditional song, which is as follows:

> *A Soul cake, A Soul cake, please good missus a Soul cake,*
> *An apple a pear, a plum or a cherry, any good thing to*
>   *make a soul merry,*
> *One for Peter, two for Paul, three for him who made us all.*
> *God bless the master of this house and the mistress also,*

And all the little children that around your table grow,
The cattle in your stable and the dog at your front door,
And all that dwell within your gate, we wish you ten times
more.
The streets are very dirty and my shoes are very thin,
I have a little pocket to put a penny in,
If you haven't got a penny, a halfpenny will do,
If you haven't got a Halfpenny, then God bless you.
Go down into your cellar and see what you can find,
If your barrels are not empty then we hope you will be
kind,
Indeed we hope you will be kind with your apples and
your beer,
And we will come a Souling no more till this time next year.[3]

To hear this song please see the reference and web link in the resource section.

In return for the song, the *"Soulers"* would be given food in the form of small *"Soul Cakes"*, which in turn gave way to other food items and hot drinks. On receipt of the 'treats' the *'Soulers'* would then pray for the souls of the dead, the more *"Soul Cakes"* received the more dead were prayed for, as each cake represented one specific soul. You will find an original Soul Cake recipe in the food section of this book.

From the rites of Souling to the obvious Trick or Treat aspects hidden in the "Punkie Night" tradition and rhymes, there is no doubt that making mischief, guising, treating and even scaring are foundations of the Halloween festival. So, next time you dress up in your finest Zombie attire or send the kids out Trick or Treating, spare a thought for the possible origins of the practise, and that you are participating in something far more ancient than the attempts of sweet manufacturers to make us part with our hard earned cash.

For the most part the above represents the majority of symbols pertinent to Halloween, but of course there are several others.

---

3. Traditional English

Although many of them do not represent actual traditions they instead correspond to attributes identified with the season itself. For instance Halloween has its own set of colours, primarily orange, which surprisingly has nothing to do with pumpkins but instead represent the orange and reds of autumn leaves as they prepare to fall from branches. The remaining symbols and attributes are normally black or dark purple in colour and are associated with decay and death and anything else generally morbid or gross. The addition of severed limbs and gore is a relatively modern rendition of the continuous death and decay theme, and all things that serve to scare us senseless. And that perhaps is the key word; to scare. Everything about Halloween is scary by its very nature, and it has no intention to be anything other than scary, it makes no apology for it.

Halloween invokes the imagination, sparks primal fears of when the dark-time of the year actually was dangerous, and human survival really did hang on a thread. It is a time when we confront the dead. To this day social norms are suspended and we are permitted to behave out of the ordinary, and indulge ourselves in merriment and feasting. In fact we behave no differently to our ancestors; we attend social gatherings where we share food and good company in the guise of parties. We celebrate the dead and the world of spirits and ghouls; we inadvertently participate in ancient rituals and ceremonies. We continue to mimic the begging traditions expressed as Trick or Treating. In actuality the only thing that has changed is the fact that to the majority it is not a religious or spiritual festival, yet many do embrace both aspects of the season, and bring it screaming into the twenty first century as a valid festival applicable to modern life.

PART 2

RESURRECTION
The Modern Face of Halloween

When imps cause pumpkins to blink and grin,
Till we in fright must run along,
Nor pause to record the chant like din
Of spirits in their Halloween song.
(Early 20th century Halloween postcard)

The mists of time part and we are transported to the modern day and the current practises of Halloween, on the surface they may seem different, but in reality and at their core, they continue to reflect a tradition steeped in centuries of history and practise. Welcome to the modern Halloween, a time of year that captures the ancient spirit that permits us to be different, not only in the way we look but also in the way we behave, Halloween is a state of mind! This peculiar festival entitles a perfectly rational suited man in the city to descend into the madness of contradictions, to dress up, to cross dress, to adopt a persona that is not his own, to be someone else for the night, to indulge in mischief and general naughtiness, to laugh in the midst of terror and enjoy a jolly good scare.

In the Islands of Britain late October heralds the short days and long, dark nights. The seasons turn to greet winter and with the turning back of the clock the afternoons become increasingly dark. Perhaps it is something firmly entrenched in our cultural consciousness that causes people to want to gather during this time, to seek comfort and warmth or even solace as the days shrink, and the darkness sings triumphantly. The coming months are the reign of darkness, the sun barely strong enough to melt frost stricken windscreens and frozen branches, offers little in the way of comfort or security. Yet humans have always gathered during these times, to feast and celebrate that which has gone before and the abundance of the harvest, yet trepidation grips the spirit as the coming darkness instils a sense of fear and lethargy even in the bravest or jolliest person.

We are no different from our ancestors of two thousand years ago; all that has changed is focus. Even today we are at the mercy of the elements and the merciless powers of nature, which gave rise to the original Halloween in the first place. A glimpse at mankind's coping mechanisms proves that we are indeed no different to our ancestors. November and December 2010 saw unprecedented snowfall across the majority of the United Kingdom, no big deal I hear those who occupy the snowy regions of the United States, or the entire northern section of Scandinavia, but we are not so used to it, caressed as we are by the warming Gulf Stream, we are naturally temperate and wet. But the manner by which society responds still expresses the inherent fear that we hold for the approach of winter. Although the worries are perhaps different in nature, people still fear the cold, dark days. Can they afford the heating bills, will they be warm enough? Will the aged and vulnerable actually survive the winter? Many, even in the 21st century will succumb to death's call. Society may have changed over the years, but insecurities and the human need to feel warmth and comfort; whilst continuously acknowledging fear continues to be expressed through the feast of Halloween. Nothing, in fact, has really changed.

Celebrations and festivals bring about a sense of togetherness, households glisten with welcoming lights, which temporarily cause the darkness to flee before them. The warm glow of Jack O Lanterns call to the dead, even if we have forgotten this fact, at its very heart Halloween perpetuates the wonder and beauty of mythology and tradition. We may not need to understand why we do these things, and we may not be able to fully articulate why, but somehow we 'feel' that they are right. As the sweet smell of freshly baked gingerbread and hot pumpkin soup rise from kitchens to tickle the senses, as screams peel through neighbourhoods; something in it all makes us feel good, it is as if we are remembering something long forgotten.

The evolution of Halloween over the centuries is in itself a remarkable feat of preservation and achievement, the fact that we still celebrate something that is perhaps thousands of years old, is a fact worthy of celebration in its own right. Central to its survival is a key fact, evolution. Halloween is not a stagnant tradition but rather one that has continuously adapted to the needs of the people and the relationship that they have with the world around them. To the original creators of Halloween, the Celts, it arose in response to the time of year, to the culling times, the cold times, a time of fear and sacrifice. The people of Britain and several millions in the United States are still those people, the Celts survive in their descendents, the people haven't changed but their environment has, and with it the face of celebration and feasting.

The modern Halloween continues to perpetuate and express a sense of togetherness, warmth and the ideologies of a perfect utopian community brought together by a single need; to survive the coming winter. We may on the surface feel safe for we will not starve owing to our commercially driven modern society, but we still continue to fear the cold of winter. People fall ill, life can become a little bit more difficult, and invariably people will also die. Halloween expresses all of this and to some it does so very consciously, to the majority it is subconscious, they do it because it feels good.

Through its evolution *Samhain* progressed into the medieval Christian festivals of the dead and of All Souls, slowly that progressed into the feast of Hallowmas; celebrating the harvest and the dead. The early twentieth century saw a different aspect; postcards heralded the coming commercialism of Halloween, a venture that would progress into the American Halloween explosion of the latter half of the twentieth century. In the United Kingdom, rural communities of the late 19th century and early twentieth continued their ancient customs which eventually were to fizzle out as a consequence of the Second World War. The frivolous nature of feasting was not encouraged in such difficult times. The 60's and 70's saw an increase in interest on both sides of the Atlantic, the British stuck to their Swede's and turnips, and children were encouraged to dress up as spirits and take to the streets, as they had centuries earlier.

The following decades saw an increase in effort with decorations and lights adorning more and more houses and commercial properties. Gardens resembled cemeteries, trees would be attired with plastic corpses and severed limbs, spiders and ghouls, spirits and pumpkins galore would ensure that the modern face of Halloween, and a demonstration of its effective perpetuation, would be firmly entrenched in modern society. Without even realising it, ordinary every day people would reach back through the mists of time, through Christian and Pagan traditions to ensure the survival of a festival in a manner applicable to the modern age. The spirit of Halloween having survived millennia of change and transformation is as strong and vibrant today as it was in the golden ages of the Celts. It may not be practised the same, but that is ok, it's evolved and that is the key to its wellbeing.

Perhaps the greatest influence on modern Halloween lies in an area that would have been quite alien to our Celtic ancestors, global commercialisation. In the United Kingdom Halloween now rivals the festivals of Easter and Christmas, and the experts at *Planet Retail* claim that Halloween will prove to be the third most lucrative trading period for British retailers.[4] In 2010 it was estimated that the British Halloween market was worth a staggering £280 million pounds and in all likelihood took a significant amount more. The range of products available in 2010 when compared with 1980 is tantamount to incredible, from a menial display of practical joke kits, fake blood, plastic masks that served only to cut into your skin and cause you to sweat like a Banshee, to the plethora of goods taking up two if not sometimes four rows of shelving in a typical supermarket.

Supermarkets responded to the increase in Halloween's popularity by supplying the public with every possible Halloween related product, limited only by the restrictions of the human imagination. Yet, the British market continues to pale in significance to our cousins across the Atlantic, but nobody can deny that

---

4. Source: Planet Retail. www.planetretail.net

the British response is quite incredible. Many will argue that the commercialisation of Halloween is unnecessary and may even belittle a feast that was sacred to our ancestors, however we live in a commercially driven society and nothing we do can remove that fact or lessen its impact. People do not have to buy into the commercialisation but invariably they do, as it somehow placates and satisfies some need within us that drives the human imagination to continuously express its creativity and connectedness. It is estimated that the average person will spend £40 on Halloween items but not including food and drink or a costume, primarily the money will be spent on a Pumpkin or several Pumpkins and other decorative items.

The internet now provides a host of British based companies, some of which specialise entirely within the Halloween sector; this remarkable commercialisation has further enabled the industry to spread its influence far and wide, ensuring that even the remotest British communities can partake in the festival. In stark contrast to the drive behind the Christmas season which is almost entirely geared towards children, Halloween has a definite adult orientated face, the children have their place, but increasingly this is becoming only a small aspect of the Halloween feast. Most adults will attend a Halloween party or event of some description as will children, although seemingly the activities of children seem to have become limited to the early evening Trick or Treat tour at dusk, with perhaps a party thrown in for good measure. The adults on the other hand tend to enjoy a feast that can be elongated to several days, some attending several events.

The confectionary industry wasted no time in jumping on the Halloween band wagon and creatively invented a plethora of sweet delights disguised in the most ghastly of Halloween shapes, from body parts to zombies, blood to guts. As a consequence other food companies responded appropriately providing a myriad of food products geared for the Halloween season. Again we come full circle; to our ancestors the act of coming together and sharing good food and drink in warmth and with good company lay at the heart of the season. Today we do the same, the feast itself is mimicking the importance of the Christmas feast, the act of sharing sustenance and comfort with those whom we love takes precedent over the occasion. Many of us may have forgotten why we do this, but that does not alter the fact that we are partaking of something far older than we can imagine, and that makes it special, it makes it important, and every October 31st we reiterate its value and worth.

Shops and online businesses abound with costumes, masks, fake corpses and ghouls, gravestones and autumn related products to an extent that can be quite baffling to the ordinary shopper. It evidently expresses the love the public have for this festival, a little joy and warmth, tinged with fear before the coming of the winter and the approaching lights of the Christmas season. Like it or not, Halloween is something that can scarcely be avoided in the twenty-first century, it seems likely that the festival is here to stay, having been resurrected from the ashes of heritage and tradition, it is not something that can be ignored or avoided with ease. However, owing to its popularity it seems that the general population has enthusiastically embraced the growth of Halloween, and will carry it screaming into the future.

THE JOY OF TERROR

Halloween provides a peculiar dichotomy of emotions, on the one hand it is filled with fun and frolics, with treats and delicious food and company, yet it also boasts a darker side and it makes no apology for it, it instils a sense of nervousness, fear and terror. How these contrasting emotions combine so well without cancelling each other out or clashing antagonistically; is probably best left to a psychiatrist to ponder, but it nevertheless causes intrigue. Ancestrally it seems that the darker aspect of *Samhain* was not something that was hidden from the young, but rather expressed right in front of them, perhaps it was wise to educate the young in the realities of life, survival and the inevitability of death, whilst they were young enough to accept these things as normal. Children are remarkably resilient and contrary to popular modern belief do not need sheltering from the truths of life, in fact they are more likely to handle them better than adults in a more matter-of-fact kind of way.

The spookiness that surrounds Halloween, the ghouls, goblins, zombies and living dead owe their existence to the ancient Celts, and the belief that the veils between worlds were at their thinnest. Not only did these spirits frighten our ancestors they also taught that fear was essential to survival, we need fear in order to cope with the tribulations of life and the reality of death. Everything within the ancient and modern expression of Halloween that is either spooky, sinister of just plain gory is an expression of the human desire to cope with death. All seasonal festivals are in fact coping mechanisms, not only do they mark the passing of the different seasons, but they demonstrate our ability to respond to change and transition. Halloween arriving as it does at the cusp of autumn and winter expresses the dying of the year as it prepares for the long sleep ahead, it is akin to death. As a consequence our seasonal creativity increased as we developed subtle rituals to enable us to make sense of the world around us, and of that greatest mystery, death. Not only are the ancestors honoured during the Halloween festival, but the constant presence of the dead, the fearful and the downright spooky serves to show us that we ourselves are fragile and one day will die. In the midst of death however, we are alive, and the relentless presence of the dead remind us of the wonder of life.

When we sense wonder or awe, when we are inspired; the common human response is to create something and to gather together with other folk and celebrate. We do this all the time almost without realising it. Our lives are filled with ritual, and these rituals help to make sense of the world around us and our place within it. We gather for Sunday lunch at mum's, why, because we are programmed to believe that this is comforting, that it makes everything seem ok. We cast spells, yes spells, by blowing out candles on cakes during birthdays; an early form of fire magic and spell casting. At Christmas time we bring a tree in from outside and decorate it, think about that for a second, a tree, from the woods, indoors! It's crazy, but still a ritual that connects us to something ancient and magical. Our lives are actually filled with far more rituals than we are actually aware of, and Halloween is no different.

The psychology of Halloween is interesting for it provides us with the opportunity to not simply imagine the macabre but to actually come face to face with it, or at least representations of it. This is an old form of magic that stretches back to the dawn of humanity, the act of making something that represents our fears, not only provides us with a manner by which to explore it, but also enables us to look at it more closely and as a consequence deal with it. Halloween teaches children that it is ok to be afraid, that fear to a degree is healthy, but it also enables us to be creative, to reach down into the core of imagination and make manifest that which only moments before did not exist. On this night all bets are off, we can be what and who we want to be, we can let go of inhibitions and scream in terror at the mere glance from a fake zombie.

The stiff upper lip of the British is slapped from our faces on this one night of mischief, terror and suspense. Halloween is at its core a coping mechanism; it causes us to look at that which we fear the most, to acknowledge the dying of the year, and to be reminded that the supernatural and the dead are never truly out of sight. Halloween also provides an opportunity for children (and adults) to become the monsters that they in turn may fear; it is an effective form of reverse psychology.

Whether or not we acknowledge the roots of Halloween does not matter, for it cannot be disputed that it is firmly entrenched in our cultural consciousness. We may not share the same fears as our ancestors, cosily sheltered in our centrally heated homes, but somehow we still enjoy and seek to be scared out of our wits. In a world where so much horror and suffering is real, where the threat of terrorism is not just fantasy, Halloween allows us to express some of the fears that we have in relation to the real world in a safe, controlled manner yet maintaining that sense of peril. As a consequence of this another facet evolved into the modern face of Halloween that our ancestors would not recognise; the Haunted Attraction Industry.

CREATING FEAR

Those of us born during the latter three decades of the twentieth century are no strangers to that peculiar of attraction; the haunted house! I would imagine you can remember the visiting fairground with its rickety ghost train, or the haunted attractions that appeared along the tourist strips of Britain's seaside resorts. Some wooden panelling, a few ragged cloths, glow in the dark props, some sound effect and a dodgy cart on a pair of rails and voila, you have yourself a scare attraction. Albeit they are somewhat improved nowadays, the old fairground rides of the seventies and eighties did have a certain charm. They were new; they promised the visitor the permission to scream their lungs out with no fear of seeming foolish. They also captured the feeling that is Halloween, and maintained that emotion the whole year round, a place that is created, just a simple construction yet dark enough and good enough to instil terror into the hearts of most riders, whilst simultaneously invoking a sense of joy and laughter, even if only in hindsight!

From travelling fairgrounds to the permanent theme parks; the haunted attraction was popular beyond expectations, and found themselves to be fixed features within any attraction park. With the rise of Halloween's popularity the theme parks responded by creating nights specifically designed for the Halloween audience, with a general horror theme these creations have compelled theme park owners into investing more and more hard cash into creative Halloween entertainment. Whereas normal October numbers in any British theme park would be low, the addition of Halloween themed nights has vastly increased the volume of customer's intent on being scared out of their senses, and encouraged to part with their hard earned cash.

Halloween events at theme parks increasingly use advanced multi-media technologies, including film and television effects to vastly improve the horror experience. Most parks will boast several "Haunted Houses" which consist of walk through mazes that resemble film sets in style and quality. These structures provide a labyrinth for a steady stream of punters to journey into the heartland of terror whilst being bombarded by a myriad of effects aimed to dazzle, surprise and terrify.

In 1991 the Universal Orlando Resort in Florida initiated their popular Fright Nights to the delight of visitors. Utilising their talents for filmmaking and special effects they ploughed the way forward and inspired the uprising of thousands of haunted attractions throughout the United States, and ultimately across the pond in Europe. Eventually Universal, having cornered the Halloween market, set the standard in theme park scare attractions. Now known as *"Halloween Horror Nights"* the event has become a world leader in Halloween event hosting, and boasts one of the largest, heavily invested festivals on the face of the planet. Perhaps inspired by the fact that Christmas is no longer a one day feast, but something which stretches to take over an entire month or more, Universal Orlando Resort and others like it ensure that Halloween can also be enjoyed over a 5 week period, that takes over the entire month of October and the beginning of November.

Across the Atlantic, the British theme parks have taken inspiration from their cousins in the USA and adopted the same Halloween tactics; the main players continue to be the Alton Towers resort and theme park in Staffordshire and Thorpe Park in Surrey, both operated by the Merlin Entertainment group. They have become forerunners in establishing and inspiring Halloween themed events in the United Kingdom. Following the influence of American theme parks they host interactive events that include haunted attractions, scare zones and walkthroughs where actors are employed to instil further fear into their customers.

Consequently the Halloween haunted event has broken free of its theme park restraints and like a wild animal on the loose has infected the country. In 2010 no less than 200 haunted attractions were present during the month of October in the Island of Britain with farms and other tourist attractions cashing in on the Halloween season and its increasing popularity, blended with the insatiable human desire to be scared witless. Cleverly almost all attractions effectively split their operations to appeal to both children and adults alike, providing early evening events tamed down for children to enjoy and indulge in organised trick or treating, to adult only affairs a little later in the day.

Children of course provide adults with an opportunity to participate in Halloween style traditions and rituals, and themed events at parks and attractions encourage this. The Walt Disney World Resort in Florida have a long established tradition of hosting their "Mickey's Not So Scary Halloween Party" where children are encouraged to dress up and enjoy music, fireworks treats and frights in a delightfully safe environment. Their British counterparts have adopted similar themes to welcome children and adults alike.

Perhaps the most peculiar modern development in the Halloween genre is the ever increasing rise in what are commonly called "Home Haunts", a term which describes the phenomena of individuals and families transforming their own homes and gardens into haunted attractions. The public are subsequently invited to visit the property and be entertained by the resident's efforts in providing a suitably chilling Halloween atmosphere. This concept has been popular in America for some time but numbers are increasing in the United Kingdom as the Halloween bug takes hold. Award schemes have been developed for the most popular attractions with stiff competition arising as a result, with frequently outrageous and incredible displays vying for the attention of the awarders.

Many may find all this somewhat distasteful; the blatant commercialisation of what is in essence a sublime and sacred ancient festival. But, it serves a purpose and a valuable one at that, it serves to ensure its survival. And ok, many may not be aware of what hides beneath the surface of Halloween or what inspired the rise of horror based attractions, but books like this serve to enlighten those if they so wish. We don't need to know what is at the heart of something to enjoy it, but knowing a little about it can only improve and accentuate the love we already have for it.

In addition to the above elements of creating atmosphere and peril; the movie and television industry has also contributed greatly to that sense of terror that we have become accustomed to during the Halloween season. The effect of this industry is obvious on the behaviour and attitudes that society develops in relation to Halloween; enough studies have been conducted over the decades to demonstrate this effect. The moving image caused the human imagination to revel in terror and horror without feeling threatened or unsafe, except for perhaps the odd nightmare or two as a result.

In British society the generation born during the sixties and seventies have images of Christopher Lee and Vincent Price firmly entrenched in their imagination. These images are powerful in that they concrete our fears and also our opinions of what is scary or not, they also identify mythologies and characters in a manner that is visible. Since the dawn of the silver screen and the first appearance of Bela Lugosi and Boris Karloff adopting the roles of Dracula and Frankenstein, the image is set; we finally knew what these creatures looked like. This added to our fears and contributed to the way we interacted with them. There is probably no doubt that the original Vlad the Impaler or the Dracul family members did not wonder around rural Romania wearing a purple, satin lined, black cloak, a widows peak hairstyle and fangs. But thanks to the movie industry we now believe that image, it is real. Our fears and the manner by which we respond to them have been programmed by the movies and TV images that were bombarded at us during our early, influential years.

The movie industry quickly took advantage of its influence and exploited the human desire to be scared witless. It was only a matter of time before the season of Halloween was used as a launch-pad for the release of horror or supernatural related movies. However there is no evidence to suggest that the earliest horror films of the 1930's had any connection to Halloween; nearly 40 years would pass before they became entwined. Perhaps the most remarkable and influential movie in relation to Halloween, was the release of John Carpenters "Halloween" on the 25th October 1978, just in time for the seasonal festivities. This movie was unique from the plethora of Hollywood productions that preceded it, mostly in that it dealt with a killer, not just a supernatural, mythical character. It also took the concepts of Halloween with all its traditions, up until that point, and exploited those too. It proved an enormous success and spawned a series of sequels and ensured that Halloween and the horror, scare industry went hand in hand. The public imagination had been grabbed and tied up screaming, and it wanted more! The industry obliged by producing more extreme forms of horror, many of which continue to be released or re-screened during the Halloween period. The publics thirst for blood and frights has increased exponentially, so much so that audiences of the old Hollywood horror classics would not believe their eyes.

Younger audiences do not miss out either, they too are entertained by the likes of the Harry Potter series, the Worst Witch and an abundance of other spooky or supernatural related programming, books, comics and magazines. Horror and the supernatural provide a means of escape from the humdrum of daily life, their ultimate association with Halloween was inevitable. However, the rise of multimedia forms of scary entertainment not only capture the spirit of Halloween, but also perpetuate its survival, like them or not, they have done more to influence our perception of Halloween, and to some extent the manner by which we practise it, than we give them credit for. Add to this the myriad of social networking sites on the World Wide Web, Halloween fan pages, groups, information and educational pages that can be found with a simple click of a mouse, Halloween is here to stay and is evolving and developing with every year that passes.

THE LAND OF HOPE AND GORY

There is one country which can be held entirely responsible for the resurgence in the practise of Halloween, the United States of America. Almost every country which partakes of, or has adopted Halloween traditions takes their inspiration from the United States. Although in colonial days Halloween was not celebrated much in the States, some folk from the British Isles continued their customs of apple ducking and snapping, and young girls would perpetuate the divinatory traditions of the season, but the largely puritan society prevented more than it permitted.[5] However the continuous increase in immigration ensured that America became a cultural hot pot, with each incoming immigrant bringing along another old tradition, another seasonal practise. Predominantly the Irish were responsible for the future of Halloween in America, the discovery of a large, orange American fruit, the pumpkin meant the old turnip or Swede could at last be rendered to the stew pot, and the ancient Celtic custom of vegetable lanterns took off in a big way. The Hispanic culture brought its own version of Halloween influence and the reverence for the dead. Add all this to the European cauldron of traditions and something quite remarkable bubbled to the surface.

---

5. Kelley; Ruth Edna. *The Book of Halloween.*

America has never claimed that the roots of Halloween arose from that land, its Celtic origin has never been disputed, but the communal expression of Halloween is entirely inspired by the American popular culture. The fact that many British folk, to this day, believe that Halloween is an American import serves only to display their ignorance for a cultural tradition that is their own. America on the other hand took the various community based traditions, and over the space of around two hundred years transformed what would have been locality specific traditions into a national obsession.

Every single culture that arrived on the shores of America brought with them their folk traditions, magic and customs. These were not necessarily aspects of their religious practise but rather traditions which were applicable to the people, to the land and to the cultures that arose there. Hence Halloween is a feast that can be practised by anyone regardless of their religious persuasion; after all it is no longer a religious event, but rather a colourful celebration of culture which naturally includes the ancestors. The unique American environment and the declining influence of the puritans ensured that by the end of the 19th century, Halloween was indeed becoming a part of annual traditions. The cultural stew pot also ensured that the ancient practises of spell casting, divination and communication with the dead continued to be an integral part of Halloween.

Various circumstances imprinted Halloween on America, the arrival of German, Polish, eastern Europeans, the British and Africans brought unique customs and traditions. The potato famine in Ireland forced over one and a half million new people into the States, each one bringing family practises and traditions from the Celtic motherlands. With the rising of colonies, the formation of states, a new country was born and with it new ways of doing things. Perhaps more importantly is the American spirit of celebrating freedom, integrity, dreams, hopes and ambitions that make seasonal festivals such a vital part of their culture. The American dream did not start well, they struggled to survive and thousands lost their lives in the pursuit of a better life, but with persistence and determination they succeeded.

Seasonal feasts arose in response to their successes, the land was honoured, relationships revered, the ancestors remembered and recalled. From Thanksgiving to Labour Day, Columbus Day to Halloween, this spirit of celebration enabled a nation to grasp old traditions and make them applicable to the new world.

America spawned an industry that embraced tradition and celebration, by the beginning of the 20th century manufacturers were making and importing party products specifically designed for the Halloween feast, which by now had become a national holiday.[6] Costumes, decorations and special effects were widely available as the years progressed. The practise of Trick or Treat, influenced by the Celtic world soon became a firm tradition of the American Halloween. Its reach was not restricted to the lands of America; it soon made its way back across the ocean from where it had originated, to a land that had forgotten its own customs.

Halloween will always be seen as heavily American, and it has every right to claim responsibility for successfully preserving it. The influence of the States cannot be ignored in the modern sense; they deserve a tap on the back for doing a job well done. They have succeeded in combining the magic of *Samhain*, the mystery of All Souls and the frivolity and frights of Halloween in a manner that is positive, inspiring and creative. Without America, Halloween may well have been lost to the mists of time.

DRAGGED SCREAMING...

...into the twenty first century, the Islands of Britain have embraced the enthusiasm of our cousins in the States, and are currently creating their own modern traditions, whilst simultaneously reaching into the past for inspiration. With a plethora of ancient customs hiding in dusty old archives and with the resurgence of Paganism and the practise of *Samhain*, Halloween is firmly on the road to a glowing, vibrant future.

The entertainment industry in the United Kingdom is also responding to the demand of the public and their insatiable hunger

6. RavenWolf; Silver. *Halloween: Customs, Recipes and Spells.*

for all things Halloween. With more and more retail outlets dedi-
cating shelves of space to this holiday and the increase in revenue,
it is likely that Halloween will only rise in popularity and scale. We
are yet to see the variety of dedicated shops and attractions that the
USA enjoys, but slowly and surely the wheel of change is turning
and bringing Halloween home.

However Britain is not alone in this resurgence.

When Halloween broke free from its origin in the Celtic nations with the mass immigration of Irish citizens to the United
States of America, it did not stop there. A seasonal force of such
vigour cannot, and will not be restricted to one location. Although
the festivals origins, as we have seen, can be traced back to the
British and Irish Celts, the central themes that fundamentally gov-
ern Halloween are multi cultural. Death and it significance is pertinent regardless of language or location. The magical quality of
Halloween to have survived adversity, social and political upheaval,
the mass movement of a people, and its survival and adoption by
various countries, is a testament to the power it has over the human
imagination.

Needless to say that several countries have in recent years
adopted the popular American face of Halloween and incorporated
them into their own harvest or fall festivals. This has not negatively
affected their own cultural observations, but simply added another
angle to them.

The twenty first century face of Halloween that we are all so
familiar with, is a blend of Celtic, British and American influences.
The world which we inhabit has become steadily smaller; traditions
can develop quickly and be incorporated into mainstream society
in a short space of time. However, with the establishment of American popular culture and the development of American theme
parks, such as Disneyland, the popularity of Halloween is increasing worldwide.

In **Europe**, certain countries have never partaken of the Halloween festival, **France** for instance has lacked any feast at the end
of October. But in recent years an American styled tradition is
emerging, thanks mostly to the presence of Disneyland Paris and
the influence of the media. However the public expression of the

festival is limited to the immediate Disneyland area, several attempts to introduce Halloween into everyday French life has been met with little support. Consequently the delightful sound of *"Trick or Treat"* (in French we may add!) is not a common sound amidst Parisian streets.

Germany has seen an upsurge of modern traditions, and is a remarkable resource of Halloween related products. Whilst Jack O Lanterns can be seen aglow in German streets, it is mainly due to the influence of popular culture. However the German Theme park *"Europa Park"* has gained significant press by hosting its increasingly popular *Terenzi Horror Nights*, which operate during selected dates in October. With worldwide recognition for a truly remarkable Halloween event, the *Terenzi Horror Nights* have placed Germany firmly on the Halloween map.

The typical **Austrian** celebration of Halloween is heavily influenced by its German neighbours, who themselves adopted the popular American format. The tradition of Trick or Treat is becoming popular but is by no means a common occurrence. However the towns of Retz and Pulkau hold an annual pumpkin festival called the *Kurbisfest* which has also evolved into a Halloween parade. The emphasis is not so much on ancient traditions here, but rather an opportunity for the family to gather in celebration of the harvest where the pumpkin is the centrepiece or symbol of the season. This feast called locally the *"Ein fest fur die ganze familie"* is increasing in popularity.

However, the Austrian's also celebrate "Allerheiligen" a Christian feast to remember the Saints and is invocative of the Catholic feast of All Souls and All saints. It is celebrated on November 1st and is an official holiday. Far from the secular celebration of Halloween this is indicative of the nature of Halloween to swim between the secular and the sacred.

Tradition holds that Austrian's would bake an "Allerheiligenstriezel", which consisted of a plaited loaf made of a soft yeast-dough, sometimes covered with large grains of sugar. This honours the ancient tradition of cutting ones plaits off as a sign of mourning. As with many customs associated with Halloween, the outcome of the baking was seen as an omen. If the "Striezel" comes out well, it is a good sign; if it burns or does not rise it is seen as a bad omen for the year to come.

"Allerseelen", another roman-catholic feast, is celebrated in Austria on November 2nd. People remember the dead and pray for them and ask that their suffering in purgatory would be eased. Here we have vestiges that resemble the Celtic feast of *Samhain*, as this was the day when the dead could escape from the liminal lands between the living and the dead, for one day only. It was customary for villagers to bake "soul bread", as offerings to be placed on the graves of their ancestors. This mirrors the Celtic practise of "Soul Caking". Candles, called "Eternal Lights" were lit on graves to guide and soothe the spirits of the dead.

Throughout the Germanic regions there were rules to be observed at home. People had to be careful of sharp objects, particularly knives, and one had to take care that no knife was placed with the sharp side of the blade turned upwards. If this was the case it was believed that the souls of dead ancestors had to ride upon it. Hearth fires were sustained and kept burning day and night to provide lost souls with warmth. Similar to the Celtic nation's bread and milk were left on tables as offerings in the hope that the dead would receive sustenance during their short regress from the liminal worlds.

In Scandinavia, Sweden's recent "Alla Helgon's dag" mirrors the Catholic feast of All Saints and the honouring of departed ancestors. Yet the typical Halloween celebrations throughout Scandinavia are again influenced by popular American culture.

To venture further afield we find Halloween superimposed, or blended into indigenous celebrations that honour either the harvest or the dead. Although in some countries the feasts of the dead such as the Chinese Ghost Festival or the Japanese O'Bon festival are orientated towards ancestor honouring, they are held during late summer, but evidently demonstrate the importance of ancestors within various cultures. The Mexican *"El Dia De Los Muertos"* is perhaps the most vibrant feast celebrated by an entire culture; this will be explored in the following "Day of the Dead" section. What can be deduced by any study of worldwide Halloween traditions is that nearly every culture who participates in it, do so in addition to any indigenous festivals that pertain to the sacred nature of Halloween. The influence of Halloween's rebirth in the United States and its subsequent exportation can be seen in almost every country who has adopted the feast.

Owing to the mass exportation of Halloween from the United States, many critics have questioned its authenticity or its purity as a specifically Celtic event. This is an irrelevant argument, its purity is not and has never been in question, in fact nothing can in essence be entirely pure, as stated before, to survive one must adapt. The same is true for seasonal celebrations. Halloween is natural for it invokes natural cycles; it is forever growing and developing weather at home or abroad. Whichever country adopts it or incorporates it into their current culture assists in its perpetuation, and that in our opinion is a good thing. The Celts have in fact, inspired the world.

PART 3

A HALLOWEEN COMPENDIUM

DAY OF THE DEAD

Men say that in this midnight hour,
The disembodied have the power,
To wander as it liketh them,
By Wizard Oak and Fairy glen.
(William Motherwell 1797 – 1835)

Too often we are sheltered from the reality of death; we confine our elderly to nursing homes, where they await the coming of the Reaper. The sick are subjected to the indignity of hospital beds and strangers who tend to them in a conveyer belt fashion. Then ultimately as we breathe our last, as the sharp edge of the sickle falls, we are unceremoniously despatched to the Mortuary refrigerator, there to await, like in a demented departure lounge; our unarranged appointment with the earth or the furnace. There, our mortal remains succumb to the silence of destruction, we finally return to the elements from which we came.

Perhaps our ancestors would find our modern methods of disposal somewhat disconcerting; in comparison they would have every right to feel a little appalled by our current attitude to death and the dead. Increasingly we have become a sanitised world, where the impending inevitabilities of life must somehow be hidden, shoved away, out of sight and out of mind. What was once a person that we loved, cared for, would hug and interact with; upon breathing its last breath becomes an object of disdain. We no longer care for the deceased, neither do we accompany them on their last journey towards the grave, instead we entrust their physical remains into the hands of complete strangers. Why?

The manner by which we deal with death is dictated by the society and culture that we inhabit, and in the Islands of Britain, we conform to the standard Victorian practise. For the past 110 years we have continued to treat our dead with the typical Victorian attitude initiated by the grimly entitled "Mourning Queen". The strict, rigorous, bordering on bizarre rituals that captured the spirit of bereavement in no way honoured the deceased, but instead pacified society that the bereaved (generally the Widow) was acting according to the standard grieving programme. This standard form of grieving, although not as rigorously observed today, continues to influence the British and to a lesser extent the American way of death. We seem to have forgotten the relevance and significance of the dead on our lives, or have we?

Nothing in life is truly forgotten, nothing vanishes entirely, and those things which are relevant remain in our social practises and rituals, Halloween is such an example. In various countries around the world the Halloween period coincided with the annual observation festival normally called "Day of the Dead". The most prevalent and active being the *El Dia De Los Muertos* festival of Mexico, the day of the dead. This observation, the lighting of lanterns on graves and the making of offerings to the dead is not a morbid practise; in fact it is quite the opposite. Neither is this practise unique to Mexico alone, and it certainly did not originate there, it is a feast that the community has strived to keep alive, and have succeeded in doing so. With its perfect blend of indigenous and Roman Catholic practise it captures the colours, feeling and pageantry of the ancient feast of *Samhain.*

Our modern Halloween practises still retain elements of ancestor honouring and the acknowledgement of death, we haven't truly forgotten the meaning behind the guts, gore and gravestones, it just hides behind a veneer of plastic. When we scratch at the surface of Halloween what we find is something so compelling, so wondrous that we cannot help but fall in love with it even deeper. For hidden beneath the squeals, the rubber rats and severed latex heads is a festival that not only venerates the dead but celebrates the effect they had and have upon our lives.

Halloween perfectly blends many traditions together, and it does so in a manner that is not religious but simply observational, sincere and genuine. It is a festival that combines the profane with the sublime in a non antagonistic way, the frivolous and the profound swim together, neither seeking to drown the other. So when it comes to our modern 21st century Halloween, surely it can be more than just a party, right? We may have lost the practises that our ancestors partook of, but does that mean we cannot invent or recreate modern Halloween traditions? Of course not, we are still those people and our deceased loved ones still impact on our lives through memory and stories. Bringing them back to life for one night during the year is an act of honouring them, and of acknowledging the impact they have had on our lives.

So, what has all this really got to do with the modern Halloween you may ask? Well, perhaps there is an ulterior motive here, a book gives one a voice, provides an avenue by which an author can disseminate an opinion or a viewpoint. So in this case the deal is this – let's put the dead truly back into Halloween! After all it is their festival.

The association with the dead at Halloween is very obvious; everything about it has a sinister, morbid, deathly appeal, and having now read the first part of this book you know why. Halloween is the only indigenous, culturally specific festival of northern Europe and the Americas that is still practised to this day, and although its expression is mostly frivolous that does not imply that it has not another level of meaning. Our seasonal festivals are vitally important to us as a culture, for they express our ancestry and heritage, they identify us as a people from a certain landscape, and they sing of our connection to the past and the manner by which we reach forward into the future. When the Irish brought their *Samhain* festival over to the newly established United States, they retained its practise for it brought them together; it connected them to something important. The same is true today. When we celebrate Halloween we are connected to our ancient ancestors whether we are conscious of it or not.

To reinvent a "Day of the Dead" would not in any form alter Halloween to its detriment, the opposite would be true. It would give our celebrations another layer, not a new one, but one that truly invokes the origin of this most ancient of festivals. This combination of the frivolous with a profound sense of reverence can be seen in the Mexican festival of the dead. The dead truly are a focus for the proceedings, the cemeteries burst into life as lights of various kinds sear through the dark nights. Table settings, meals, snacks and treats are laid out as offerings to the dead. Breads are baked in the form of corpses; sugared skulls are painted in glorious Technicolor to represent the continuous influence of the ancestors on our lives. After all, we are their sum totality. Following this reverence for the dead, the living will gather in joyous celebration of community, family, friends, warmth and merriment. What is expressed in Mexico no doubt reflects some of the ancient practises of the Celtic *Samhain* celebrations, blended with Aztec mythology and the later adoption of Christianity. We may have lost aspects of this in Britain but that does not mean that we cannot reclaim it. We are quick to give up our cultural practises and traditions for the sake of misguided political correctness, but why should we? It is a sad fact that many Britons believe Halloween to be an American import, not realising that it originated here in these islands, so many years ago.

This chapter seeks to inspire you to create new traditions that sing of the old ways, of the traditions of our ancestors, many of which can still be found in dusty old archives and libraries. Every region throughout Britain had its own unique Halloween traditions, each one of them an echo of the past. A little digging in the history books can reveal much about the rituals of your ancestors.

A religious mind or a spirituality is not a requirement for remembering our dead, they are and always will be a part of us, setting aside a day once in the year to recall them, to honour them is just as valid today as it was 2,000 years ago. One does not need a religious conviction or belief system to acknowledge the importance and significance of our ancestors.

So why not have a go, perhaps you are looking for a new angle for your annual Halloween bash, or maybe you seek to educate your children into the dual aspect of the tradition. Perhaps you lost someone during the previous year, and are still grieving, or maybe, just maybe; you feel something more than just the frivolous and would like to do something else, something different that highlights the antiquity and relevance of Halloween on our modern lives.

Many believe that traditions are things that were initiated in the distant past, this is not entirely true, for in actuality 'We' are the initiators of tradition. We can begin at any point in time to set a precedent, to create new traditions and practises that are relevant to our family group, our friends and communities. We do it all the time, mostly without thinking of it consciously, from family gatherings to the Christmas feast; they are all rituals and traditions that someone in our families made relevant. They created a tradition. Similarly in one of the authors' community the focus of Halloween as both a time for fun and frivolity and an opportunity to recall the dead and visit their graves is already a long established tradition.

The dead are always with us, they are only truly a relic of the ancient past when we forget them. Next time you pass a typical British cemetery, stop and take a look, except for some of the newer graves the majority will be neglected, in a state of disrepair. Yet the names upon those tombstones may well share the same surname as yourself, the bodies beneath now rotted to become a part of the earth, are the flesh of those who lived where you live. They had lives, they grazed their knees as children, they cried, fell in love, led ordinary lives much like our own, the only thing that separates them from us, is time and death. One of the authors was reminded of this connection during the photo shoot for this section of the book, the cemetery we visited was crammed full of graves inscribed with the surname "Hughes". These were Kristoffer's ancestors, a part of his story. For that reason alone the dead are worthy of acknowledgement, for we are the people we are today because of them. Bringing back a direct and conscious focus on the dead during Halloween deeply honours the roots that we have to place and to community.

If you recall in the first part of this book it was explained how the ancient feast of *Samhain* was celebrated over a period of 3 nights, and the same can be true today. In fact many members of the Neo-Pagan community have totally embraced both the sacred and fun filled aspects of *Samhain*/Halloween and extended the feast to its traditional 3 nights. The Mexican feast of the dead is also a festival that extends over several days. Now in my mind that is permission enough for the rest of the western world to do the same! Imagine it, 3 whole days of celebration, the day before Halloween, followed by the 31st of October itself, then the 1st of November; all Hallows Day, *Samhain* Day. Within this period, similar to the Mexican celebrations; a period can be set aside which is reserved specifically for honouring the dead.

Why should our cemeteries be devoid of attention? Why should they be gloomy and lifeless during the dark turning of the year? There is no reason. We have long forgotten the rites of the dead and the fact that they are deserving of our reverence and attention, but it can change with acknowledging a day in the year that is entirely theirs. It isn't new, it isn't original, it is something our ancestors practised for thousands of years and is as relevant today as it was then. This is why we have a Halloween.

During the nineteenth century numerous Irish and British villages continued the ancient Celtic tradition of leaving offerings for the dead. Lights would adorn cemeteries, tombstones would be cleaned and scrubbed, the grass trimmed and tidied for the coming winter. There is no evidence to suggest that this practise in any way mirrored the elaborate rituals of the Mexican Dia De Los Muertos tradition, but none the less the emphasis on Halloween and the dead was firmly entrenched in the popular imagination. But something happened as the world became smaller and people migrated, their traditions diluted, cultural melting pots influenced holidays and seasonal activities, but not so much to their detriment. The practises may have changed but the festival remained. Halloween was not something that could easily be removed from societies of a Celtic ancestry.

Halloween purists may scorn at the fact that many of the modern symbols have more in common with scenes from a gory horror movie than with an ancient festival. To those folk we have a simple message 'lighten up', it's not all bad, and the guts and gore still retain within them elements of the sacred and sublime. They are symbols which express the dead and the threat of death. The manner by which they are utilised during Halloween simply demonstrates the coping mechanisms that modern mankind has developed to deal with the mystery which Halloween represents.

As the Western world developed, mortality rates decreased significantly with improved sanitation and health care, and death no longer gripped society in its merciless grip as people lived longer. But, death could not be eradicated from Halloween, and when it did return it emerged from the silver screen. The vampire and serial killer, monsters and malevolent spirits became the accepted face of Halloween. Death was something that was deemed not suitable for commemoration, instead only the gory and terrible are celebrated as a remnant of Halloween's deathly associations.

Only a century or so separates us from the traditions of our ancestors and perhaps for many they bear no relevance on modern practise. They do however influence our practise and as you have seen demonstrated in this book, our current traditions have within them ancient Celtic and Catholic DNA. So bringing the dead back into Halloween isn't new or different, we simply resurrect these practises and make them relevant to our modern societies. Perhaps we in the west have for too long compromised our own traditions for the sake of political correctness and conformity, Halloween provides us with the perfect opportunity to preserve aspects of our ancient past, in a manner which is honourable, enjoyable and fun.

Invoking the Past

So, perhaps you fancy bringing actual ancient practises into our modern celebrations, giving an authentic edge to the event, nothing could be easier. Including aspects of old traditions and rituals into your Halloween not only honour the ancient roots of the festival, but also brings something different into it. Most folk are happy to just go with the modern trends, with the traditions that they themselves have created, however more and more people enjoy bringing other, older elements onto the proceedings. We can go over the top, if there is such a thing, with our decorations and props, dazzling our guests with amazing recipes and ghoulish food and drink, but sometimes bringing in something else makes the event more memorable. Below you will find a few brief suggestions, little elements of the old world to bring into the new.

- Create a new family/community tradition by visiting the graves of your loved ones, or memorials to those who died during war, accident or disaster. Light grave candles or other forms of lighting whilst taking offerings of autumnal foliage and carved Swede's or pumpkins. Spend some time preparing the graves for winter, trim the grass, dispose of old flowers, clean the tombstones, replace old or damaged memorial containers.

- Spend time making Gingerbread Corpses and Coffin biscuits as offerings to the dead, involve the kids, take the finished cookies to the graves of your loved ones together with candles and other forms of autumnal illumination. See recipe section for further instructions.

- For 3 nights over the festival, one night before, the night of the 31st and the evening of the 1st November, as dusk falls light candles (safely) in every window of the house and keep them burning until you retire. This mimics the tradition of guiding the spirits of the dead to the warmth of your home.

- Set up a table or shelf in the main party area of your home and festoon it with framed photographs of your dead loved ones, ask your guests to bring photos along too. Let your imagination go wild, have it on various levels adding height, candles, fake tombstones, coffins, and make it a focal point where the dead are truly present.

- As a centrepiece to your party table have a cauldron, real or plastic filled with a fruity punch, cider or other equally festive beverage. Prior to beginning the feast encourage everybody to take a glass of punch and hold a toast for the departed, call your ancestors by name and ask that "May they be remembered".

- The evening before Halloween or the night after invite a select few friends over for a "Dumb Supper" this rather odd, yet powerful tradition calls for the guests to bring memories of their dead, i.e. photos, and partake of a meal that is eaten entirely in silence. It goes against normal dining practise and feels 'weird', but it does bring the dead to mind, after all it is their festival. Traditionally the centrepiece of the table is a bowl of grave dirt.

- Spend an hour or so baking "Soul Cakes" (See recipe section) with your children or friends and recite the history of them. In modern neighbourhoods it is becoming traditional to take a few "Soul Cakes" to your neighbours on Halloween morning, explaining that they are to be eaten in honour of the dead.

- Hold a "Mourning Tea" with echoes of the ancient 'Souling' tradition, either at home or hire a grand old hotel or hall, encourage guests to dress in their finest Mourning attire for Afternoon Tea, sombre music and feasting. Incorporate some of the above into the event; be limited only by your imagination.

- Encourage your community or neighbourhood to participate in a Halloween candlelit procession at dusk, journey through the streets to your local cemetery to lay flowers and candles on the graves of your ancestors.

- Instead of the typical pumpkins, why not carve an abundance of Swede's and turnips and other traditionally British root vegetables. They are much trickier to hollow and carve but the potential for unusual and spectacularly ghoulish creations are endless. See instructions in decorations section.

The above serve to simplify the old traditions of Halloween in ways that are easily incorporated into your modern practise. But look to your own locality, library and archives and discover other traditions that may have been specific to your locale that you may be able to resurrect, and involve your family and friends or indeed your entire community. The possibilities for Halloween related frolics are potentially endless.

FRIGHTS, LIGHTS & DELIGHTS
Creating Atmosphere

By pumpkins fat and witches lean,
By coal black cats with eyes of green,
By all the magic ever seen,
May luck be yours this Halloween.
(Early 20th century Halloween postcard)

At the heart of every Halloween celebration is the art of decoration, creating a suitably scary, eerie and atmospheric environment for your guests to enjoy. Nothing shouts Halloween better than a suitably haunted home, a place that sends chills down the back of your guests and cause them to squeal in delight. The ritual of decorating is imbedded in the human psyche, it is something we have always done, from ancient times mankind has used colours, paint, crafts to bedeck the halls during the seasonal festivals, and we continue to do so to this day.

Decorating our homes creates an atmosphere; we send out signals that something important is taking place, something that warrants our attention, time and effort. The scale of decorating is limited only by your imagination and the bounty of your wallet! Some folk will scour the shops and the internet for that perfect addition to their Halloween decor, whilst others are happy with homemade haunted creations, or simply a carved pumpkin or Punkie that takes pride of place in a window or on the hearth. Arguably the efforts of home haunters during the Halloween season have increased in the United Kingdom in the last ten years, with some houses rivalling the Christmas efforts. Although not quite on the scale of our American cousins, we Brits are getting there, with more homes illuminating the night with ghoulish lights and impressive displays.

Creating a suitable party atmosphere for your Halloween feast need not be a daunting task; regardless of your budget we have something to inspire you. Being old hands at the Halloween Decor game we are conscious of financial restraints and with that in mind we offer a variety of ideas to suit every pocket.

As avid readers of Halloween books and 'How To' guides, we realise that to be faced with studio quality photographic presentations can be a little, if not entirely off-putting. There have been numerous occasions where we have glared longingly at the epitome of Halloween, portrayed in a fabulously lit, perfectly constructed photo and thought "I'm never gonna be able to do that!" The truth of the matter is that to even attempt to replicate something from a fancy book or magazines is no easy task, for our environments differ entirely, with that in mind we have set out to be a little different from your run of the mill Halloween book.

What we have presented here is as honest and genuine a portrayal of the love we have in creating these things, they are not fantasy. The props are our own, the set pieces are our own, all the environments portrayed are real, no studio has been used. Everything you see has been created, cooked, made, stirred, shaken or lit up within the confines of our own homes, our gardens or our local landscape. Hopefully what we will have achieved and convey to you is a sense of authenticity.

We know how difficult it can be to come up with new ideas, to add that certain something to an event, and with that in mind we try and simply inspire you to find new ways of doing things, new materials to use and so forth. We hope that you will in no way be daunted by what follows, but rather see them as possibilities, little creative snippets from which you can take your inspiration from. By all means use all the elements in the photographs, or just take a few of them and adapt them to suit your own haunt. Some elements such as lights or incidental background items or materials do appear in the following suggestions; all of them will be explained and noted.

Cost is always a factor when it comes to creating a scene, for those who have the luxury of money being no object the task is straightforward enough and anything is possible (not that we are bitter!). But for the majority a budget has to be taken into account. Nowadays there are plenty of discount outlets that can be used to add the odd effect or two, with a myriad of cheap, cheerful, yet effective items for sale. Even the tackiest bag of cobweb for less than a quid can be made to look amazing with just a little advice and a little imagination. The 'grab it cos its cheap' mentality is a common

Halloween curse, but don't be led into thinking that one must dash into the nearest £1 store or supermarket and blindly cast all Halloween items into a basket, give it some thought. You would be amazed what you can make, arrange or conjure up that will give your haunt the spook factor this Halloween.

The following suggestions have all been individually rated, in a very un-British fashion we may add, we could not find a carved Punkie clipart therefore the following is subject to our quintessentially invented "Pumpkin Rating!" The rating ladder comprises of 1, 2 or 3 pumpkins. They are representative of:

☺ = Easy, cost effective, needs little time or effort.

☺☺ = Moderate effort required with moderate cost, sometime needed.

☺☺☺ = Tricky/Challenging, modest cost, significant time and effort required.

Suitably Haunted

Chucking a few decorations around the place is fine, but getting it to look good is another matter, the space that you have, whether it be your home, office, the local school or community centre is the canvas upon which you set your frights. Making it truly terrifying requires your thinking cap, a whole hoard of fluorescent, bright lighting is not only going to illuminate every flaw in your decorative attempts, it also going to be a bit of a let down to the throng of people who are expecting a chilling atmosphere. To create the best environment, and one which is suitably haunting, bear the following three simple, yet important points in mind:

1: Lights. Nothing is worse than a floodlit haunting. Simple lighting effects will transform your entire haunt into a place truly fit for the dead. Daunted? Don't be, it is much, much easier than you imagine. By all means if you can afford the best ultraviolet lights available, and a hoard of professional lighting systems, go for it. But, if like us your budget does not quite stretch that far there is still much that can be done.

- **Candles** – easily available and ranging in price from the ridiculously cheap to the expensive, candles will totally transform your haunt. Bunch a whole load of night lights in holders on a windowsill or table with a few pillar candles thrown in for good measure, and you have an impressive display. Add further ghoulishness to your candles by melting red wax crayons either in a double boiler, i.e. a glass bowl over a pan of boiling water, or by gently inserting the tip of the crayon into a naked candle flame, the red drips will add a bloody effect to your ordinary candles. At Halloween one cannot have too many candles, put them everywhere, use anything you have that can hold a small pillar candle or a night light, the effects can be staggering as they cast flittering shadows and lights onto your walls. As always, common sense should be in place, there is nothing worse than being patronised, but you know the score, don't leave them unattended and make sure they will not fall off anything.

- **Low Wattage bulbs** – the 40 watt mark is a good effective way of lighting the night, they are significantly dimmer than your average living room bulb, and come in a range of colours for added effect. Alternatively buy a few small pots of glass paint and colour some plain bulbs. Avoid using overhead lighting in any shape or form, but rather go for accentuated lighting, lamps, lanterns etc, items that can be smuggled into corners and dimmed, shades can be covered in fabric to dull the brightness from any lamp.

- **Jack O Lanterns & Punkie's** – Whether they be pumpkins, real or fake, turnips or Swedes they add a dramatic and atmospheric light effect to your haunt. How many should you have? As many as your wrists can tolerate carving or your pocket stretch, you can never have too many! The illumination of these need not be entirely by candle light, there are a vast array of battery powered pumpkin lights available to purchase, or pop a couple of glow sticks in for good measure, they will last the duration of the night and combining colours can be very effective. Where should you place them? Anywhere! On windowsills, by the hearth, next to the door, on the porch, in the garden, bookcases, shelves, tables and stairs, any suitably flat surface will suffice.

- **Electronic Fairy/String lights and Rope lights** – Thanks to the internet and the Garden Centre, these items are available all year round, and many companies will sell the typical Halloween colours of orange, green, blue and purple. Some of the large popular multi-goods internet businesses have these items at low prices to suit most budgets. If you have anything that will oblige and stay still for any length of time, then cast a few fairy/string lights over it; lay them high so that their twinkling lights will cast reflections on the ceiling. The perfect place for an orange or purple rope light is in the guttering, along the base of walls or fencing. The trick with Halloween lighting is subtlety, hide them, push them into corners or under bushes, it's the glow of lighting that creates an effect. Unlike Christmas, where everything is bright and in your face, Halloween is much subtler, hidden lights imply hidden mysteries, ghouls and things that go bump in the night.

- **Novelty Lights** – We have all seen them, most of us have attics full of them! The tacky glittered skull with internal lights that accommodates a few batteries. The plastic vampire head with glowing red eyes, the candelabra made entirely of aged bones which flicker in the night. They are tacky, but we love them, they add an element of fun and silliness. If you have them use them, they add atmosphere just as much as anything else does.

- **UV/Black lights** – These remarkable light sources are a must for any haunt, they are available in a range of sizes and will cause anything white or fluorescent to glow as if by other-worldly light. Again depending on the depth of your wallet, you could go crazy and festoon an entire room with UV/Black strip lights. Or modesty, transform a window sill, or other small place into an ectoplasmic wonderland.

Any lighting source can be altered with a little thought. An effective way of changing the mood and quality of light is to disturb its projective ability with another material, such as fabric or smoke. Smoke machines will naturally affect light with very little effort on your part, but not everyone has a smoke machine. If you don't have a smoke machine and are unable to purchase dry ice, you can burn incense sticks near to a light source, you may need a few sticks to do the job, the smoke will accumulate and affect any lighting. One does not need to spend days creating these little light effects, although some do! Just a little forethought and a smattering of planning will have your house lit up like a Mausoleum!

2: Sound. This is painfully simple, made even easier by modern MP3 technology and downloadable material. Even the budget shops will sell CD's that comprise of haunted, spooky sounds or suitably creepy music. There are several excellent music producers which create compositions made exclusively for the Halloween season and haunted attractions, see the resource section for a list of recommended material. So what do you do with sound?

Think of the usual sounds that abound in your pre-haunted location, if it's at home, it will be domestic appliances, washing machines, etc, the TV, the sound of your central heating and so forth. The trick is to remove the usual humdrum sounds that are normal and replace them with those that alter the environment. Most households will have several music players, whether they are portable old fashioned type ghetto-blasters to the modern Hi-Fi unit or the IPod docking stations and speakers, all of them can be used to full effect. We would suggest different sounds in different rooms if possible, for instance in the kitchen something haunting and melodious, whilst in the main gathering area ramp it up with something a little livelier and perhaps a little louder. Outdoor sounds can be created easily by having a speaker in an open window or under a waterproof box in the garden, especially near the door where your guests will arrive and where the local kids will come trick or treating.

Haunting a place by sound can be a fickle business, and its effectiveness is dependent on so many variables such as height and size of the area. But, yet again, forethought is the key, play with various sounds on available music players and see which will be best suited for your environment, keeping in mind what kind of event you are hosting and who the audience will be.

Your TV and DVD player can also be used for the effective use of sound, from playing a collage of Horror movies to a single movie played on a loop, to the specialised Halloween DVD's available on the market. Make use of all the multi-media appliances you have available to you to create a chilling haunt.

3: Smell. One should never underestimate the power of smell, and at Halloween it can add a whole new angle to your haunt. Now, we are not suggesting you allow something dead to fester in a corner for that little touch of authenticity, it can be achieved with less trauma! It may be something that you have not given much thought to, but once you look around in shops and internet stores you will quickly discover that the Halloween industry has long been involved in selling smells.

So what does Halloween actually smell like? In all honesty, probably of nothing other than leaf mulch and decay, the typical smells of autumn, but we have been led to believe that certain smells are associated with certain times of the year. No-one can deny that the common smells of Christmas are cinnamon, nutmeg and exotic spices, yet most 21st century homes do not smell like that in reality. As for Halloween, the common manufactured aromas are also spicy, warm and evoke a feeling of companionship and feasting. Pumpkin has very little smell, its fragrance is dependent on spices, but a turnip or Swede with a candle inside will smell amazing, as will Butternut squash and small gourds, the vegetables literally cook by candlelight and let out a delicious smell that truly does capture the season. Bear in mind that if you are having guests over and they will be sharing in a meal or other Halloween foods, then your haunt will no doubt be full of wonderfully inviting aromas, but all of this can be further enhanced artificially.

We would suggest that you trawl your local market, shops, and the internet for fragranced oils, perfumed wax discs, sprays, automatically dispensing air fresheners, and incense sticks. When you have chosen your fragrance and the manner by which you will disperse it, place the strongest near the entrance so that your guests are greeted by a smell as well as your fantastic Halloween displays. They may not notice the smells consciously but the subconscious effect will undoubtedly affect them.

So, with the introductions out of the way, take a deep breath, grab a bottle of something strong, knock it back and pray for daylight!

FUNKY PUNKIES

A wood-store provides the perfect garden Punkie display feature. Carved Swedes nestle amongst recently collected pine cones with a couple of onion Squashes for company. The deep, orange Punkie light accentuates the burnt umbers and reds from autumn foliage. A woven basket is home to a range of artificial gourds guarded by a Punkie and a Squash, whilst candle lights flicker and glass votives cast shadows against branch and root. Old logs and branches add height to the display and a wreath of acorns glued onto a polystyrene circle adds a further festive touch to this quaint display. The ivy covered wall behind the wood-store grins in the flickering lights, each leaf smiling at the warmth of autumn. The sweet smell of heated Punkies fills the air; their glowing inner lights daring any would- be spirit to pass swiftly by!

The presence of a pumpkin, that typically swollen, orange, grinning symbol of Halloween is commonplace; in fact it has become 'The' mascot of the season. Practically every Halloween based book on the market and the plethora of websites dedicated to this festival will contain tips for growing, gutting, peeling, carving, stuffing and anything else you could possibly do with a pumpkin! We could have ventured down the same route, but we have instead chosen a different direction. Not that we are turning our back on the popular pumpkin, not at all, they will grace the Halloween threshold with equal pride to its traditional British counterpart, the long ignored and abandoned Punkie lantern!

Punkies, a carved Swede or Turnip, known to our American cousins as the Rutabaga; lovingly derived from the Swedish meaning "Root Bag" is the traditional Celtic version of a Pumpkin. As the reader you may have never carved a Swede or Turnip, or these words serve only to make your blood run cold as you recall childhood memories of Swede carving, aching wrists and stiff fingers! The task of carving a lantern, a Punkie, is no easy task, and requires significantly more effort than carving a Pumpkin. The Swede is hard, rock hard, it has no seed pocket at its centre, but thankfully, they are remarkably smaller than a pumpkin.

The markings and colouration of the Swede make for seriously sinister lanterns, and although they appear less orange on the surface, than a Pumpkin, a candle at its centre magically emits a staggeringly orange light. The outer skin of the Swede ranges in colour from deep purple to beige and pale yellow, a plethora of peculiar patterns, scars and markings provide ample opportunity for the budding carver to invoke the root's personality. The fact that the Swede is a root is what makes it so different from the pumpkin which gets to bask in sunlight and feel the elements against its orange shell. The Swede alas, is submitted to a life of darkness beneath the earth's surface; there it lingers in perpetual gloom, awaiting the farmers plucking, when finally it sees the sun. Its nature as a root makes it a creature of the underworld, its sinister appearance and peculiar light quality made it a perfect candidate for a lantern that would protect the living from the dead.

The Swede cannot compete with the size of a pumpkin, but what it lacks in stature it makes up in personality, these versatile little roots are pretty freaky lanterns. They will add another depth to your decorations and heighten the atmosphere of your haunt. Do not stop at one, they are much cheaper to buy than a pumpkin, go crazy and buy a dozen or more! Even the smallest Swede can look pretty amazing, but do bear in mind that they will not last as long as the pumpkin; they do not share the same outer shell. But with an army of carvers some petroleum jelly you will still manage to squeeze three days worth of value from the humble Swede.

For the task, and do bear in mind it is an arduous task; yet highly rewarding, you will need the following:

- A range of Swede's – Turnips
- A sharp serrated knife
- A craft knife
- Marker pen
- Metal ice cream scoop (Non-mechanical)
- An old metal spoon
- Petroleum Jelly
- Night lights
- String
- Pumpkin carving miniature saw

Begin by examining your Swede and deciding which aspect is best suitable for a face. Swedes have unique features which differ greatly from the uniformity of a pumpkin. Once you have found the best place for its face, draw the features directly onto the skin with a marker pen. Now set the Swede into a plastic shopping bag, to prevent shrapnel spattering your kitchen, and on a sturdy work surface slice a section off its bottom end to assist its standing. Remove the top section, or crown of the Swede, ensuring that you allow enough space to insert a knife a scoop or a spoon, do this by inserting the blade of a serrated knife at a 45 degree angle. This ensures that by removing the lid you simultaneously remove a good section of the Swede's innards.

Set the lid aside and with a knife begin to slice deep lines into the Swede's flesh, carve the lines close together, then slice in the opposite direction to create a grid or lattice type pattern. Now with a metal ice cream scoop, use the non-mechanical type, dig out the lattice of flesh. Bear in mind this is difficult work, the air may well be fragrant with vivid language, and the Swede may also demand that you provide it with blood (worry not, some blood will add to the final result), but hang in there, you will get the hang of it! Once the majority of the Swede is de-fleshed continue to slice at the inside edges of the root to thin the walls, alternate between ice cream scoop and spoon, whichever performs the best.

As you approach the outer skin take care not to puncture the thinning walls. When you are happy with the hollow you have created begin to carve the features. The best tool for this task is one of the miniature carving saws found in any pumpkin carving kit. Do this with care, the Swede is a delicate creature and must be treated kindly. Now push a metal skewer or cross headed screw-driver through the flesh of the Swede around a quarter of an inch from the cut open end to accommodate string for hanging, repeat directly opposite. Pop in a lit night light and replace the Swede's lid. Wait a few minutes for the candle flame to scorch the inside of the lid, remove the lid and carve the scorched section out to create a chimney.

Smear the cut edges of your Punkie with petroleum jelly to prevent the flesh from shrinking and turning brown. This will preserve your lantern and extend its life by at least 24 hours.

Your Punkie is now complete and ready to protect you from those things that go bump in the night.

Follow these guidelines for maximum Funky Punkie effect:

- Punkies look good when grouped together in large numbers of varying sizes; group them with natural wood products, logs or branches. Use artificial autumn foliage to add depth of colour.

- Fill a window sill with Punkies at varying heights using empty boxes or stacks of CD's or DVD's covered in fabric, spooky cloth or sacking. Scatter pine cones amidst the company of Swedes.

- Make an effective outdoor display by upturning a large garden container, or using a suitable table or wooden box to stack a group of Punkies. Stand them at varying heights using plant pots or stones on top of coarse straw or moss.

- If you are fortunate to have a spiked garden fence or balcony, push a carved Punkie onto each spike before lighting. Glow sticks are perfect for illuminating outdoor Punkies.

- Line an assembly of Punkies on a wall or veranda.

- Indoors, arrange a table display of Swedes grouped together with tall pillar candles, place gourds and squash of various sizes amidst the Punkies to create a festive vegetable patch.

- If you have glass fronted cabinets or bookcases place a selection of grim faced Punkies within them, for these, use the small purpose made battery Jack O Lantern lights.

HANGING PUNKIES

A small corner of a cottage garden is transformed into a grinning, glowing Punkie patch. As guests turn a corner, smiling lights gently dancing on strings end and cradled by the bare branches of a Rowan Tree, protect the living from mischievous ghouls. Branches and twigs illuminated by Punkie light transform a simple October garden into a sinister world of smiling spirits.

These sinister sentinels defy a spook to come anywhere near your home! A small tree can accommodate several Punkie lanterns, if you are fortunate to have a large tree or a selection of trees, then the Halloween sky is the limit. Hang as many as you physically can, they look incredible and the light they emit is deliciously spooky.

Simply push some string through holes punctured just below the cut end of the lantern, tie a good knot to secure the string. Decide how long the handle should be and push the other end through the flesh tying it off inside the Punkie. You now have a hanging Punkie, a "Root Bag".

The humble Swede is mightily underestimated, but we hope that with the publication of this book, you will be inspired to resurrect the Punkie and bring them glowing back into the twenty first century.

ANCESTOR TABLE

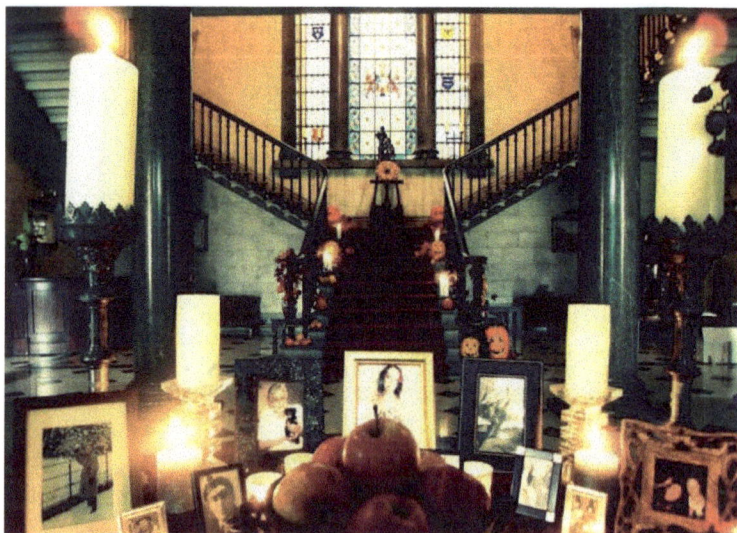

Elegant candle sticks embrace tall pillar candles that shine their light upon the dead. Ancestors smile from gilded frames as votives glisten about them. A cauldron of apples promises the gift of rebirth and of remembrance and memory. The dead, though departed are not forgotten; long may they be remembered.

Technically this is not a decoration, however an ancestor table can be something of a focal point and can be as simple or as elaborate as you like. The photograph demonstrates a fairly simple set up, even if the setting is rather grand, but let your own muse guide you. The purpose or intent of the ancestor table is not simply one of decoration, but rather a place in the house that subtly expresses the sublime aspect of Halloween. It feels more like an item that expresses the spirit of "Day of the Dead" yet can be made to suit your haunt, it may tell a story of the folk in the photographs who are no longer with you.

The ancestor table is not a glum feature, on the contrary, it celebrates the lives of those who you have lost, and what better party to invite your dead to! Why not ask your guests to bring photographs to add to the table.

Some tips for an effective and eye-catching ancestor table:

- Find elaborate, antiquated picture frames to suit the season, trawl through car boot sales, flea markets or online for unusual frames.

- Festoon the table with flowers in tall vases, black, grey and shades of deep purple work well; however a simple trick is to purchase fresh flowers from the local supermarket, florist or garden centre. You can usually find supermarket flowers that have passed their best being sold at discount. Place your flowers in a dry vase and position in a dry cupboard or room to wilt naturally. Drape the dead flowers with artificial web for a decaying look. If you wish lightly spray the flowers with a smattering of black and silver spray paint.

- Purchase tall pillar candles and place on elaborate candleholders or stand them within glass vases. Use small glass votives to hold night lights which can be safely scattered about the table.

- Place a bowl or a cauldron of apples at the centre of your table. Apples represent the Goddess Pomona whose feast day is associated with Halloween; they are also Celtic symbols of the Underworld and the kingdom of the dead.

- A table with a gothic taste can be draped in black fabrics, scatter glass beads and artificial jewels to catch the candle light amidst the photographs.

- An autumn ancestor table should have fruits of the season upon it, bowls of dried acorns to represent decay and trans-formation, fall foliage real or plastic will accentuate the table's rich, deep colours.

- In some Celtic households guests bring offerings of food for the dead which are placed upon the ancestor table, beautiful glasses of wines and liqueurs are also appropriate gifts to lie before the dead.

ECTOPLASMIC EXTRAVAGANZA

A cottage hearth, warmed by firelight and the glow of Punkies plays host to an otherworldly lustre. Vases of dark flowers glow by sinister light, spirits sing from glasses of ectoplasmic fluid, candle flame recoils in fear of the blue, ghostly radiance. The enchanting combination of ultraviolet or 'black light' and quinine drags an otherwise cosy living room screaming into the night.

This effect will have your guests gasping with surprise, they will wonder how you created such a dazzling effect, yet will have no idea that it involved little effort and very little cost. Pictures can never do justice to this simple effect, but we can assure you it is well worth the little effort required. Within minutes you can have sections of your home haunt, or indeed your entire haunt aglow with a supernatural, ectoplasmic light. To create this effect you will need the following items:

- UV/Black lights
- Tonic water
- A range of vases or glass receptacles

The beauty of this decorative effect hides in a simple reaction of chemicals and light. The taste of tonic water is derived from Quinine, and it is this which reacts under UV/Black light. The reaction is instantaneous and requires no effort on your part other than deciding how to display your range of freaky glowing vases!

So, decide where your display is going to be placed, this ultimately is dependent on the size and amount of UV/Black lights at your disposal. A limited number does not mean a limited display, a single UV/Black light can be used on a window ledge or sill facing the street. Ensure the curtains or drapes are closed to contain the light and prevent its dispersion.

Gather a suitable number of receptacles to contain the tonic water and create your display, we suggest that items such as flowers be placed in the vases to accentuate the overall effect. A diverse mixture of vases and glasses in different sizes and styles will serve to add dimension and depth to your display.

Finally when you have your vases and glasses in place and you are happy with the overall look, fill them with tonic water and switch on your UV/Black lights. At this point you may need to adjust your display to gain optimum results from the light reaction.

The scope of this simple yet powerfully effective method is limited only by your imagination. Plan ahead, your guests will be mightily impressed.

HALLOWEEN TREE

A black stained branch sits in a cast iron cauldron, the glow of orange light dances from hanging ghosts and bats and tombstones, lovingly crafted with Salt Dough. Black leaves from plastic flowers glued to the end of twigs add a gothic feel to an otherwise bare and forlorn branch. A bunch of twigs dipped in vivid orange paint, gaze enviously at figures that swing gracefully from the limbs of the Halloween tree.

Why should a tree be limited just to Christmas? Halloween befits a tree just as much as its glittery yuletide cousin. Black trees are frequently seen on the Halloween market and appear to be increasing in popularity. So this year why not have a tree as a focal point for your spooky decor? This project takes a lot of time and a degree of effort to create, but we think the overall impact is worth the trouble. We have taken nature as inspiration, after all this time of year sees the trees fall fast asleep, their bare branches like skeletal limbs against a moonlit night.

Why spend a fortune purchasing a Halloween tree when you can make one yourself, in fact it can easily develop into a family tradition where a new tree is created each year. This concept can be adapted to a 12 inch tree or applied to an 8 foot beast that commands attention. The suggestions here are just a few ideas of what can be done simply and cheaply, but by all means go crazy and festoon your tree in whatever is right for your haunt.

To replicate the tree in the photo above you will need the following items:

- A good sized branch – do try to use a dead branch and not butcher a living tree!
- Salt Dough Halloween decorations
- Black spray paint
- Acrylic paints
- PVA glue
- Cotton
- Glitter
- Soil & Stones
- A vase, cauldron or suitable container.

Begin by finding a suitable branch that is approximately the right shape and size for the location you have in mind for this project. The branch may be located in your garden or you may need to venture further afield to find a suitable candidate. Wash the branch with warm water and ordinary household detergent to remove any fungi or bugs or other bacteria from it. Allow the branch to dry.

In a well ventilated area, preferably outdoors, spray the branch with the black spray paint. Cover as much or as little of it as you wish, sometimes a light spray can be just as effective. Allow the paint to dry before transferring the branch to its allocated pot, stand the branch in the pot and push soil and loose stones into the container to wedge the branch in place. You may need a few pairs of hands for this task. Ensure the branch is sturdy and not likely to fall on unsuspecting victims!

Your branch is now transformed into your embryonic Halloween tree, with this in mind study it for a few minutes and decide which parts of it may need highlighting. Consider the light source in the room, from which direction does it come from? Decide upon your highlight colours and apply using acrylic paints. Lightly smear PVA glue onto the tree and sprinkle with glitter for further sparkle.

Allow the paints and glue to dry and add lights, the small string/fairy type lights are perfect for festooning your Halloween tree. Whatever else you think may compliment the tree add it at this stage.

When you are happy with you masterpiece adorn with cotton threaded Salt Dough decorations. Finally switch on the lights, stand back and tap yourself on the back for a good job done!

HALLOWEEN SCARECROW

He stands not simply to scare the crows, but to send chills down the backs of anyone who dares to cross his path. A dead branch imbedded in a cauldron forms the frame for our creepy Scarecrow. Cloth and sacking stuffed with straw form a deformed body upon which sits a glowing Punkie head. His smile is mocking, daring, he knows something we don't. Eerily brought to life, he stands as sentinel between the worlds, watching the living and taunting the dead.

This super effective and original Halloween prop captures the spirit of the season whilst costing next to nothing to produce. You could choose to make a small version of the scarecrow or go for a 6 foot monster! You will note that the suggestion here is for a Swede

– we are British after all! But the head can be substituted for a squash, a gourd or a pumpkin.

For this project you will need the following items:

- A 'Y' shaped branch
- A Swede or Pumpkin
- Garden string
- Muslin
- Sacking or other coarse fabric
- Soil
- Straw
- A sturdy base e.g. plant pot or cauldron

The trickiest aspect in creating this item is finding the ideal branch, take time to wander your local woodland to find the perfect candidate for the task. Preferably you will find a suitable dead or wind-blown branch that does not require cutting from a tree. The perfect shape is an elongated "Y", the stem of which will act as the body and the outward reaching limbs will form the arms.

Wash the branch with warm water and detergent and allow to dry. Plant the branch into a suitable pot and pack in tightly with loose stones, soil, sand etc. Find the best aspect on your branch and begin by creating the scarecrow's body. The model in the picture above is a simple combination of sacking and cloth wrapped around a little straw and then tied onto the branch; this takes some fiddling to get the right look, and of course, is entirely dictated by your chosen branch. Persevere to create a good looking body, add autumn decorations to it, cob-web, insects and birds etc if you so wish.

The Punkie head should be relative to the size of your branch to prevent it from toppling over. Although if you have been bold and gone for a ten foot branch or whole tree, then a gigantic pumpkin is more than suitable! Find a stick, sharpen one end and push into the bottom of your Punkie, the length of this stick is again dependant on the size of your branch. Push the opposite end of the stick into the body of your scarecrow to hold it firm, you may need to use wire or duct tape to secure the stick firmly.

Finally position your Scarecrow and add lights or other embellishments of your choice.

SHRUNKEN HEADS

Wrinkled skin and blood-stained severed edges frame the dull, dead eyes that stare forlornly from the severed head of an unsuspecting victim. Desiccated flesh surrounds the grim mouth locked in an endless scream. These shrunken heads add a terrifying, threatening feel to the home haunt.

These hideous little heads are easy to prepare and extremely effective, adorn a table centrepiece with a host of severed heads impaled onto spikes, attach a wire hoop and wear one about your neck. The possibilities are limited only by your sick, twisted imagination! Generally, shrunken head methods will call for using the humble apple, but we have found that the results are poor and not as effective as the vegetable pictured; the Beetroot.

The unassuming Beetroot comes in a range of sizes, and when cut into spills forth red flesh and blood coloured liquid. They are the perfect vegetable for gruesome shrunken heads.

For this task all you will need is:

- A range of Beetroots (Raw)
- Small craft knife
- Wool, string, muslin etc
- Beads, the ends of tailors pins, or Googley wiggley craft eyes

Once you have selected the finest head shaped beetroots you could get your hands on, examine each one for individual markings and scars that may highlight its features. Draw the outline of the eyes, nose and mouth onto the beet and then carve out with a small craft knife. Don't attempt to replicate works of art here; the beet will shrink to less than a quarter of its original size. An old rag or newspaper would be wise, the juice will stain. Place your carved beet in the oven at a temperature of 75'C for between eight and ten hours, depending on the size of your beet.

To dry them conventionally by way of placement on a radiator or a warm cupboard may take 4-5 weeks to shrink, so make them well in advance. Once dried use natural wool or artificial hair or straw and secure to the crown of the beet to create hair. Wrap some muslin around the head to create a hat. Arrange as you see fit. They can be used as place markers for your guests, or worn about the neck as grisly Halloween trophies or to add a blood-curdling accessory to your party costume.

Kept in an airtight container they should keep for a few years.

SPOOKY STAIRCASE

*Grinning Punkies, pumpkins and squash line the staircase lead-
ing the foolish to their final destination. Candles flicker by golden
leaves and boughs of foliage drape the banister. Autumn sings of Halloween treats in this mansion of foreboding delights.*

The chances are that your haunt will have one of the following
three, a staircase, porch steps or a hallway. Even the grandest staircase can be highlighted for the season, and you do not need an enormous amount of material to achieve an effective look. Our staircase
has been embellished with simple gourds, squashes, Punkies and a
range of artificial pumpkins and foliage. Candles simply give another dimension and quality to the light; they can be contained in
glass jars or vases if safety is an issue.

Staircases are sometimes overlooked, yet they beg for some Halloween attention. It needn't be complicated or difficult, even a range of paper votives holding a single night light or battery powered bulb can effectively transform a stair. However, you may have a hundred gourds, pumpkins or Swedes at your disposal, in which case you can completely overwhelm your staircase.

The trick is to utilise a range of carved and non carved vegetables, and add other lights to provide depth and richness to your display.

HALLOWEEN SALT DOUGH DECORATIONS

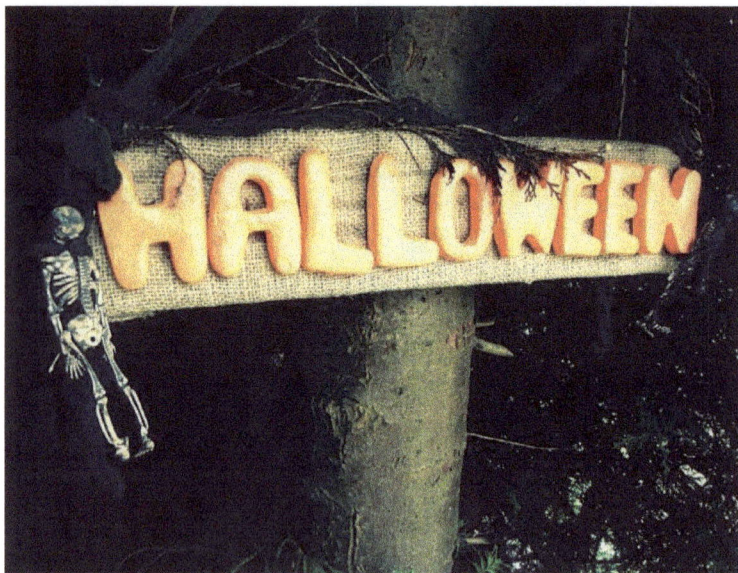

A primitive sign greets guests as they arrive at your haunt, glittery ghosts, cats and bats wait to be hung upon their festive gallows. A grinning face and a scardey-cat plaque glow with votives that hide behind them. From the jolly to the creepy, the versatile, alchemical reaction of flour, salt and water bursts into life as fabulous Halloween decorations. Varnished they last a lifetime; wrapped in ghoulish paper, they make pretty gifts for your hallowed friends.

This method of making long-lasting, personal decorations is simple, cheap and kids will thoroughly enjoy making them too. Limited only by your imagination the potential of Salt Dough decorations is endless, from small tree decorations to items that can be hung in windows to plaques and tombstones, anything can be achieved and its only limitation is the size of your oven! Get the kids involved in a craft that is easy and great fun for all the family.

The following suggestions are based on small decorations cut with Halloween themed cookie cutters, but why stop at this? Let your imagination run wild and create cemeteries, haunted house votives, coffins and corpses, in fact entire centrepieces or window sill decorations can be made completely with Salt Dough.

What you will need:

- 2 cups of plain flour
- 1 cup of table salt
- 1 cup of water
- Acrylic Paints
- PVA glue
- Googly eyes
- Halloween cookie cutters
- Glitter (optional)

To prepare the Salt Dough, add the plain flour and salt to a large mixing bowl and mix thoroughly with your hands. Slowly add the water until a firm dough texture is achieved. If the dough is too sticky add a little more flour, a little more water will moisten if too dry.

Once the dough comes away from the side of the bowl and forms a large ball, place the dough on a lightly floured surface and knead for approximately 10 minutes. The longer you knead the mixture the better the overall result. Cover the dough with a damp tea-towel or cling-film and allow to rest for 20 minutes. Unlike bread the dough will not increase in volume.

Roll the dough out to about half a centimetre thick and use Halloween themed cookie cutters to cut out various shapes. Worry not if you do not have any cookie cutters, simple shapes such as ghosts, bats and coffins can easily be cut out free hand or by cutting a template out of cardboard. If you intend to hang your salt dough decorations, make a small hole to thread the string through by pushing a cocktail stick through the dough, give it a wiggle to widen the hole.

When all the shapes have been cut to your satisfaction, place them on a greased baking tray and place in a pre heated oven at 50'C for 2-3 hours for small pieces, 3-6 hours for medium sized pieces and 6-9 hours for larger pieces. The longer the pieces have to bake at a low temperature the better; a high temperature oven will result in the Salt Dough swelling which may result in separation of the dough layers. The Salt Dough is ready when a hollow sound is heard upon tapping and they are slightly golden in colour.

When the pieces have cooled completely choose appropriate colours and paint your dough. When the paint is dry you may further enhance your decorations by lightly painting them with PVA glue and sprinkling glitter onto the damp glued surface, shake off the excess onto some paper and allow the glue and glitter to dry.

Finally add some googly-wiggle eyes; these are available in packets at craft shops and come in a range of sizes, they consist of oval clear plastic pockets with an internal free moving black acrylic piece and resemble eyes.

Finally thread decorative wire or cotton through your decoration and hang.

To ensure that your decorations preserve well, paint them in a minimum of 3 coats of strong, clear yacht varnish, making sure that every centimetre is well varnished. Without a varnish coating the Salt Dough will rapidly absorb moisture from the atmosphere and become limp and soggy.

Further ideas with Salt Dough:

- Use letter cookie cutters to cut the word "Halloween" or "Boo" from dough and bake until hard, colour appropriately and glue onto a wooden plaque or stand them freely on a shelf.

- Make haunted house votives by rolling out a flat, square piece of dough as thinly as possible. Then using a template or free hand, mark out a pattern onto the surface of the dough. Stylised haunted house patterns with several windows are most effective. Carefully place your dough on a greased baking tray and begin cutting out the shapes. Bake slowly, preferably overnight on your oven's minimum setting. To enable your masterpiece to stand unassisted, simply find wooden dowels of around 3 inches in length and push them through the dough a few millimetres from its bottom end. Once baked, painted and dry, push sandpaper into the dowel holes to smooth the edges and insert the dowels. The overall size of your piece will dictate the required length of dowel to allow your item to stand securely. Finally place night lights in glass holders behind it and dim the lights. We find that these Salt Dough pieces are best painted entirely in a matt black finish.

GLUE GHOSTS & BLOOD

Nifty little ghosties hang in gleeful splendour, these easy to make glue ghost won't cause your wallet to go bump in the night. Googly eyes shiver and shake as you pass them by, hang them near a window or a draught to see them shiver in the breeze. Glue blood drips eerily down a wall, their hues of red glistening in autumn light.

Nothing could be easier to prepare than these decorative items made entirely of PVA glue, a perfect activity to share with the kids. All you will need is:

- PVA glue
- Waxed paper or Greaseproof paper

- Googley- wiggly craft eyes
- Glitter
- Red acrylic paint (if making blood drips)

Onto a large sheet of waxed or greaseproof paper, use the tip of the PVA glue container to draw typical childlike ghosts, begin with the outline and then fill in the centre.

For blood drips simply add as much water based, acrylic red paint to the glue until the desired colour is achieved. Bear in mind that with the addition of the paint the blood drips will be more fragile than their plain, ghostly counterparts. As with the ghosts, draw the blood drips onto your paper.

Allow the glue to dry for a minimum of 48 hours, depending on ambient temperature. The glue is set when translucent in appearance. Peel slowly from the paper, add glitter if you wish, pierce the top of the item with a needle and thread if you wish to hang them. Display in windows or hanging from mantle or Halloween tree.

Another fabulous tip is to puncture the top end of glue blood drips and attach either string or decorative chain, wear about the neck as an accessory to your costume to give a 'slit throat' appearance.

PUNKIE JARS

A plain mantelpiece is transformed into ghoulish splendour with the addition of these glowing jars. Transform any corner or shelf with a range of Punkie jars in different sizes to bring a ghostly glow to your Halloween party. Never throw out an old jar when it can be turned into spectacular Punkie jar!

These pretty little jars prove how simple and cost effective many Halloween decorations can be. We all like to purchase the latest 'must have' product, but sometimes, the most effective and eye catching are the simple things that you make at home.

Delight your children in allowing them to smear old jars, and themselves in gorgeous glue! These little decorations will last years and delight your guests. For this project you will need the following items:

- A range of glass jars
- Orange crepe paper
- PVA glue
- Paint brush
- Pencil
- Marker pen
- Night lights

Clean your selected jars and remove any labels with hot water and detergent. Rounded jars are preferable for this project. Bear in mind that you are not limited by the size of the jar.

When the jar is clean and dry, cover the outer surface with PVA glue, smooth the orange crepe paper onto the glued jar making sure that the underside of the jar is also covered to prevent visible edges of paper. Apply upwards of 3 – 4 layers of crepe. Any loose edges can be smoothed down with the addition of more PVA.

Apply more PVA glue to the neck of the jar and then cover in decorative or garden string. This will ensure that the top ends of the crepe are well covered. Paint the string with more glue, turn the jars upside down and allow to dry.

When the jars are dry, draw a Jack O Lantern style face onto the surface of the crepe with pencil. Then follow the pencil outline with permanent marker pen to complete your design. To preserve your jars the entire outer surface can be sprayed with artist's varnish. Insert a night light and display.

TIP: If time is against you – use a hair dryer to help set the glue faster.

GRAVEYARD GRUB

The Gluttonous art of Feasting

Double, double, toil and trouble,
Fire burn and cauldron bubble,
Eye of newt and toe of frog,
Wool of bat, and tongue of dog,
Adder's fork and blind worm's sting,
Lizard's legs and howlers wing,
For a charm of powerful trouble,
Like a hell-broth boil and bubble.
(Macbeth: William Shakespeare)

Perhaps William Shakespeare in the verse above didn't quite have a feast in mind, but it does, none the less, conjure an image of a cackle of witches busy preparing their finest meal on All Hallows eve! After all; on the hallowed night of Halloween there is no better sound than the contented grunting of a coven grazing on fine food and beverages. The inclusion of the above verse is not present for its quaintness; we have included it for the image it invokes. A memorable Halloween feast would indeed be an act of conjuration in itself, the creating of marvellous things for the crowd to feast upon, the adorning of the kitchen in Halloween finery, the invoking of smells that charm and bewitch your guests.

A dinner party or buffet spread on All Hallows eve is no ordinary meal; it is an act of magic. Everything that we do on Halloween is in essence an expression of the season, what would otherwise be an ordinary feast or meal thus is transformed into an 'experience', something out of the ordinary. Some folk go to tremendous efforts to delight their guests, to provide an immersive, quality event that tickles the senses and teases the imagination.

From time immemorial food has brought people together, the very act of partaking in a meal defines a family, a community. The sharing of food is perhaps the oldest ritual of humanity, one which combines our need to survive and the need to share warmth, reward and sustenance. Food brings people together, it forms the central focus of celebration, it becomes the stage by which we as a community celebrate together.

We no longer exist in a 'eat to live' society, with food aplenty and where the seasons no longer play an essential role in dictating what we eat and when, we are free to express through food. When people come together, the bringing or the preparation of food defines the moment that the activities begin. We are all familiar with the rituals of seasonal food, the preparation of the Christmas pudding and cakes, months in advance, the baking of sweet goods and delicacies. The making of wines and infused liqueurs, all these things express the initiation of a seasonal feast, and something about them makes us feel good. Food and its rituals contain a memory of warmth, of celebration; it is something that connects us to the very spirit of humanity. No wonder our televisions are crammed with food programming twenty four hours a day!

The food of Halloween is as important today as it was to our Celtic ancestors over 2,000 years ago, not only does it represent, both in colour and mood the descent into autumn and winter, it also offers warmth and comfort. Going into winter with a belly full of food makes us feel good. There is something within our species consciousness that remembers vividly what it was like to not have the security of plenty. The winters were harsh, they threatened us at every turn, and other than the convenience of supermarkets, we are inherently the same people as our ancestors all those many hundreds of years ago.

No Halloween celebration would be complete without a feast fit for the dead! With that in mind we offer you a coffin-full of recipes to delight or even appal your guests. In the same manner as the previous section, the following instructions are as simple as possible and the results are easily achievable.

As authors and avid fans of Halloween we understand the limitations of budget and the fact that a good party need not cost the earth. We ourselves have created, designed and cooked, baked, stirred or conjured the following recipes with no assistance from a professional food designer, they are we hope a honest portrayal of what anyone can achieve with just a little inspiration and imagination.

We have attempted to retain a spirit of effective simplicity throughout this section, to enable the creation of ghastly delights with little effort. Halloween is a busy time, and factor in any children that may be running amuck in your household, and the time restraints are further restricted. As authors we have always been put off by complicated recipes that serve to confuse and befuddle rather than inspire. With this in mind we have attempted to simplify the following suggestions and recipes without compromising their effectiveness. So, grab your apron, dig out your finest cauldron, dim the lights and prepare to boil, toil, trouble and bubble!

HALLOWEEN AFTERNOON TEA

A Quintessential British Tradition

"A roaring fire casts an orange glow mimicking the Jack O Lantern that graces the hearth; the wood crackles and mocks the October winds that howl mercilessly at the window. The table is set for a

Halloween tea; the finest china with its gold rim glistening in the fire's glow, commands centre stage on the small lace covered table, treats bedeck the cake stand with promise of sweet delights. A knocking on the door announces the arrival of another batch of Trick or Treater's. It is a typically British scene, a warm and cosy Halloween. A tea cup rings as it meets its saucer, the warm blood within the cup almost spilling over the golden rim to kiss the blood stained lip mark on the teacups edge. With a chuckle, the resident achingly rises to its feet and meanders to greet those eager to receive their treats."

This is not a recipe per so, but rather an elaborate serving suggestion.

Nothing expresses the quintessential nature of British food culture more than the tradition of Afternoon Tea, which is attributed to the Duchess of Bedford. It is said she suffered from melancholy and lethargy, and so to improve her mood she would invite friends for afternoon tea. This fashionable British social activity took off within high society. Within a decade it was commonplace to share sophisticated tea with neighbours and friends throughout the British Isles.

However, what most folk would consider to be "High Tea" is erroneous. The tradition of tea, served in the best china with cakes and finger sandwiches is correctly called Afternoon or "Low" Tea, owing to the fact that it was served entirely on a low, round table, almost at knee level, between the hours of 3 and 5pm. High Tea refers to the working class main meal of the day, served after 5pm where the entire family would gather at a "High" table.

The tradition of Afternoon Tea is quaint, sophisticated, elegant and extremely well mannered. No longer confined within the ranks of the upper classes; Afternoon Tea is commonplace in current British society. Cafes and restaurants abound throughout the United Kingdom, serving delectable afternoon treats to the weary shopper or tourist. It may not be served with the same pomp and ceremony in the finest china, but Halloween is an occasion where traditions should be observed and honoured. It provides the perfect environment for an old fashioned gathering of friends who also get to dress up for the occasion, after all what good is fine china without a fine hat to match!

With this in mind this section of food and beverages kicks off with a typically British scene, to inspire the reader to hearken back to days of old and invite some folk over for Halloween Afternoon Tea. Some remarkably quaint china can be purchased for less than five pounds in charity shops or car boot sales. Loose tea makes the perfect beverage and will allow one amongst you, to become tea leaf reader in true Halloween style.

Why not give your friends and neighbours a truly unique Halloween experience this year by inviting them over for Afternoon Tea, in addition to your main party, after all, why stop at one social event? Ask that they come in their finest Mourning attire to enjoy tea in the company of friends and the dead. The bets are off, normality is suspended, be elegant, bring out the gothic attire, bring out the drag for that matter! Afternoon Tea may look pretty and sophisticated, but why not give it another edge. Egg mayonnaise sandwiches (crusts off, of course!) can be tinted green with a few drops of food colouring. Crust-less cucumber sandwiches can be pressed into beetroot juice to provide an edible, bloody appearance. Fairy cakes, scones or Bakewell tarts can be drizzled with delicious Grenadine for a truly gruesome look. Serve with rich, yellow Cornish clotted cream and a bowl of Bramble blood jelly (See recipe).

The authors delight in the quintessentially British, the sumptuous, sophistication of days gone by, of scenes that leap as if from the pages of an Agatha Christie novel. Marvellously British yet touched by a hint of something sinister. Nothing screams Halloween better than subtle horror, a perfect scene that on the surface seems quite normal, but look closer, scratch a little and all is not as it may seem.

Our email addresses can be found at the end of this book, so why not send us images of your finest, spookiest Afternoon Tea.

HOBGOBLIN STEAK & ALE PIE
The Unofficial Official Pie of Halloween
Serves 4 – 6 People

A wicked combination of the "Unofficial Beer of Halloween" with the best of British ingredients to create a mouth-watering, sumptuous pie to slay the mightiest hunger, deeply satisfying, this is the ultimate autumnal comfort food.

Ingredients:

- 1 kg of braising Steak
- 500 ml Hobgoblin Beer

- 3 Beef stock cubes
- 3 heaped tablespoons of plain flour
- 2 large onions
- A little cooking oil
- 2 heaped teaspoons of Dijon Mustard
- Knob of butter
- A handful of button Mushrooms
- Handful of small/baby carrots
- 1 teaspoon of fresh Thyme (1/2 teaspoon of dried)
- 1 packet of ready-made puff or short-crust pastry.

Method

Chop or cut the steak into bite size pieces. Peel and chop the onions into small chunks and fry until transparent in oil in a large saucepan.

Place the steak into the same pan until the meat is sealed. Stir the flour into the meat juices. Open the bottle of Hobgoblin, an obligatory "Swig" is mandatory at this point, and slowly pour into the saucepan with the meat and onions.

Add the beef stock cubes to the mixture and continue to stir. Add water if the mixture is too thick until a desired consistency is achieved. Add the Dijon mustard, the Thyme, Carrots, button Mushrooms and continue to stir gently until boiling. Reduce the heat and allow to simmer for approximately 1 hour and 30 minutes.

Follow the instructions on your pre-prepared pastry and cut into your desired shapes, place on a greased tray and cook in the oven at 200C until golden. Once cooked, serve your Hobgoblin Steak and Ale pie on a hot plate or dish and place the pastry lid on top.

Alternatively – for a moister pastry topping, place the steak and ale mix into a lightly greased oven proof dish, and cover with a pastry lid. Cut a vent hole in the centre of the lid. Bake in a pre heated oven at 180C for approximately 20 minutes or until the pastry is crisp and golden.

Serve with chipped potatoes and garden peas.

TIP: If time permits – make this the day before and leave covered in the saucepan overnight. The following day add a little more Hobgoblin and re-heat. This will allow the flavours to develop and intensify.

PUMPKIN PIZZA

Serves 4-6 people

Pizza is a firm favourite for most, so this Halloween why not create a ghoulishly delightful Pizza that will impress your friends and befit the season. This recipe is easy to prepare, and can be made entirely from scratch or easily recreated from shop bought dough or pizza base.

Ingredients

- 500 g bag of Bread flour,
- 600 ml warm water
- 7 g sachet of yeast
- Salt
- Tomato puree
- Red Leicester cheese
- Black pitted olives

- Olive oil
- Chilli oil (optional)
- Cardboard, scissors and a pen.

Method

Add the water to a large mixing bowl together with the yeast and salt. Stir thoroughly.

Add the flour gradually until a firm dough is achieved. Add more flour if the dough is too sticky more water if too dry. Knead the dough for approximately 5 minutes.

Smear some olive oil around the inside of the bowl to prevent the dough from sticking as it rises. Place the dough into the bowl, cover with a damp cloth and leave to rise in a warm room or cupboard for a minimum of 2 hours.

After the dough has risen remove from the bowl and knock the air from it. Cut the dough into 3 balls which will eventually become your pizza bases.

With a rolling pin roll the dough to your required size, this recipe should adequately yield three 12 inch pizzas with a medium crust. Once the dough is prepared cover the surface with tomato puree. Now grate the cheese and sprinkle over the top according to your own taste.

Draw a pumpkin face onto a clean piece of cardboard, an empty cereal box works well. Cut out the shapes for the eyes and the mouth. Place this template just above the pizza. Using the black pitted olives fill in the spaces which you have cut out of the cardboard. Once you are satisfied remove the template to reveal a Jack O Lantern pattern on your pizza.

Sprinkle the pizza with salt and pepper and add the chilli oil if you so choose. Place in a pre heated oven at 200C for 20-25 minutes.

TIP: If you don't have time to make the dough, shop bought is perfectly adequate. If you are not a fan of olives substitute them for chopped pieces of Pepperoni.

KITTY LITTER SURPRISE

Serves 8-10 people

A dish that will literally turn your guests' stomachs upside down, yet have them chuckle in bemusement. See what the Witches cat left after the Halloween party. Dare you use the scoop?

Ingredients

- 2 packs of sandwich biscuits e.g. custard creams
- 1 pack of chocolate fudge finger bars
- 1 packet of digestive biscuits,
- 1 large sponge cake of your choice or chocolate rolls
- Yellow and green food colouring
- Ice-cream
- 1 NEW Cat Litter tray and pooper scoop.

Method

Thoroughly wash the new cat litter tray and scoop. Break up the cake and add to the litter tray. Try using a cake which is moist and contains cream, butter-cream and or jam to avoid the dish being to dry.

Place the sandwich biscuits into a plastic bag and smash with a rolling pin, ensure that some of the pieces are left as sizeable chunks. Sprinkle the biscuits over the cake base.

Place the digestive biscuits into a bag and smash those into grit size pieces. Pour onto the biscuit and cake base. Carefully open the yellow food colouring and sprinkle onto the biscuits in defined patches to resemble urine stains. Flick some green colouring amidst the biscuits in light patches.

Take an entire packet of chocolate fudge finger bars, place on a plate and microwave them for no longer than 5 – 10 seconds until the chocolate is malleable not melted. Quickly transfer these to the litter tray and arrange in a revolting display of faecal deliciousness. Bend some of them, smear one onto the edge of the tray, in other words use your imagination to be as disgusting as you possibly can.

Place the scoop into the tray and set as a centrepiece on your buffet table. Serve with lashings of your favourite ice cream.

SEVERED FINGER WRAPS

Serves 2 people

Halloween would not be complete without some severed digits festering in tortilla wraps, with that in mind, try our take on what makes a good finger sandwich!

Ingredients

- 5 Sausages of your choice
- 6 Tortilla wraps
- Red food colouring
- Flaked almonds
- 1 Roll of Bandage

Method

Place the sausages in a preheated oven set at 180C and cook until lightly golden.

Cover the bottom third of the sausages in a Tortilla wrap and trim to create the effect of a bandaged digit. Use the bandage to tighten the wrap around the sausage.

With a sharp knife make small incisions at the top of each sausage and gently push in an almond flake, these may be coloured if you so wish to resemble nail polish. Once this is done – serve on a plate or board and add some drops of red food colouring to the bandages to give a bloodied look. Serve with Graveyard Mash and sides of tomato ketchup, barbecue sauce and mayonnaise.

TIP: To save time, microwavable sausages can be used or hot dog type sausages.

GRAVEYARD MASH

Serves 6-8 people

This is a great dish and a simple recipe if you are struggling for time and have a few guests arriving for your party. It can be made proportionately to the size of your party simply by multiplying the following ingredients to your own requirements. Served in a large pasta type dish this makes an impressive centrepiece for the dinner table and will have folk gasping in amazement. All our recipes are easily adaptable, so be inspired and let yourself go; your Graveyard Mash is limited only by your own despicable imagination.

Ingredients

- 6 Tortilla wraps,
- 10 large potatoes
- 2 large red onions
- 8 Sausages
- 1 tablespoon brown sugar

- 2 tablespoons of red wine vinegar
- 1 tin of mushy peas
- Instant gravy granules
- Butter
- Pinch of Thyme
- Half a cup of milk
- Salt & Pepper
- A pinch of Rosemary

Method

Remove the Tortilla wraps from their packaging and place on a clean surface. Cut out various tombstone shapes, the number of which is dependent on the size of your serving dish. For a large 8 person dish around 10 – 15 tombstones will provide a fantastic effect. Place the cut out shapes under a medium grill and toast until golden brown on both sides. Remove and allow to cool on a wire rack.

Peel and cut the potatoes into chunks and place in a large saucepan of boiling water. Add some salt and allow to boil for 45 minutes or until soft.

Whilst the potatoes are cooking, slice the red onions into small chunks and place into a frying pan of hot olive oil. Cook until transparent then add the brown sugar and red wine vinegar, continue to stir until the mixture resembles a pleasant, sticky consistency.

Place the sausages in a preheated oven at 180C until golden. Ensure your kettle is filled and boiled at this point in preparation for the gravy. Warm the mushy peas in a saucepan over a medium heat or warm through in the microwave following the instructions on the tin. When the potatoes are cooked the race is on! Remove them from their pool of boiling water, add milk, butter and the Thyme and mash thoroughly. Drop half the mixture into a large serving dish to resemble an island in the middle of the dish put the cooked sausages on top and cover with the remaining mash. Smooth down the top of the mashed potato island and quickly add the toasted tombstones. Drop a small dollop of the red onion sauce in front of each tombstone and adorn with sprigs of Rosemary to create a spooky graveyard setting (You must be relatively quick in your graveyard construction to prevent the dish from becoming cold).

Quickly make up the instant gravy and pour around the potato island along with the mushy peas, any onion sauce you have left can be plopped into the wet mixture. Dim the lights and serve!

BEANS ON GHOST

Serves 2 – 4 People

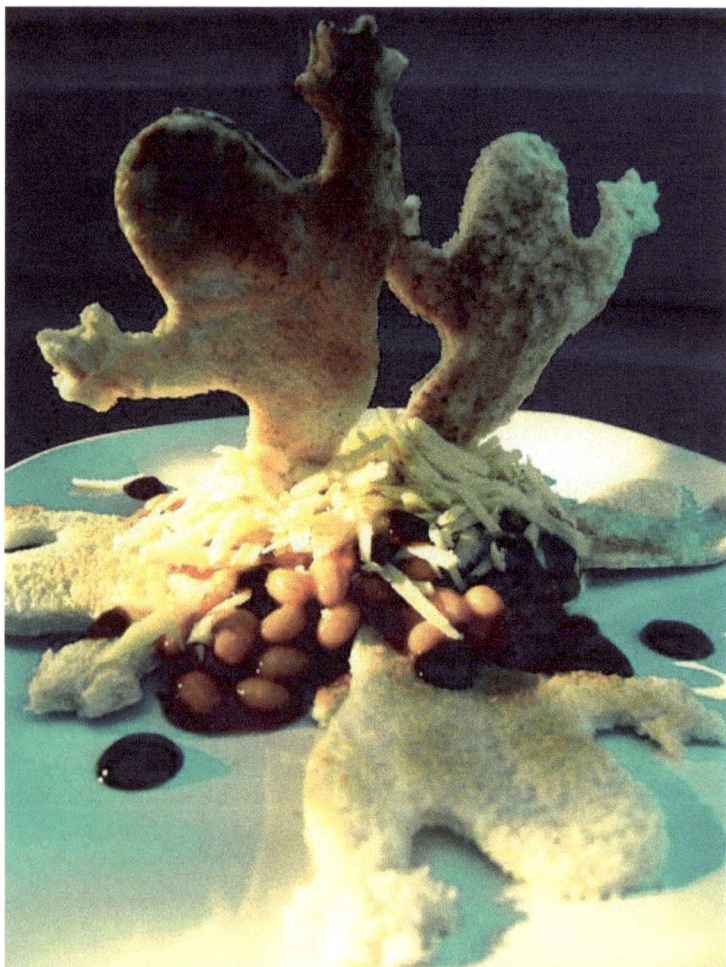

This is a great way to start Halloween morning for kids and adults alike. Start the festivities with a surprising breakfast presented in true Halloween style, preparation is minimal and the dish is simple to prepare but bound to impress.

Ingredients

- 1 loaf of bread
- Can of Baked Beans
- Cheddar cheese, grated
- Brown sauce

Tools

- Halloween themed ghost cookie cutter

Method

Toast the bread and with a cookie cutter firmly press out a number of ghost shapes. Grate some cheddar cheese. Place the beans to warm in a saucepan over a medium heat or in the microwave.

Arrange some of the ghosts in a suitable pattern on a plate. Take the warmed beans and serve a small amount into the middle of your ghost toast. Add a small tower of grated cheese and anchor further ghost toast into the cheese and beans. Squirt with brown sauce and serve.

SOUL CAKES

Serves 10 – 15 People

"A soul cake, a soul cake, please good missus a soul cake! An apple, a pear, a plum or a cherry any good thing to make us merry!"

Nothing is more traditional at Halloween than Soul Cakes, not only do they represent the seasons Hallowed past but they taste delicious too. They are great with Halloween afternoon tea, snacks between feasting or to hand out to bemused Trick or Treaters.

Ingredients

- 150 g of Butter
- 200 g of caster sugar
- 550 g of plain flour
- 2 egg yolks
- 1 teaspoon of mixed spice
- 5 tablespoons of currants
- Pinch of saffron (optional)

Method

In a large bowl cream the butter and sugar together until soft and fluffy, then slowly beat in the egg yolks. Gradually fold in the flour and add the spice and saffron. Continue to fold whilst adding in the currants. Carefully add the milk a little at a time to make a firm dough that comes clean from the side of the bowl.

Empty the dough on to a floured surface and with a floured rolling pin roll the dough to a thickness of approximately a quarter of an inch. Use a 3 inch circular cookie cutter to press out the cakes. Place on a greased oven tray and pop into a pre heated oven at 200'C until golden brown.

CORPSE COOKIES

Makes Approx 20 cookies

Gingerbread corpses make an ideal cooking project for kids who will thoroughly enjoy decorating them too. Ideal as snacks or to take to the cemetery as offerings for the dead, these little corpse cookies are easy to prepare and look perfect for the season.

Ingredients

- 350 g of plain flour
- 175 g of light brown sugar
- 1 – 2 teaspoons of ground ginger
- Half a teaspoon of ground cinnamon
- 1 teaspoon of bicarbonate of soda
- 1 egg
- 100 g of margarine
- 4 tablespoons of Golden Syrup
- Writing icing

Method

Combine the flour, ginger, cinnamon and bicarbonate of soda in a large bowl, add the butter and rub together thoroughly. When fully combined, add the sugar, the egg and the golden syrup and combine to form a stiff dough.

Empty the dough onto a floured surface and roll out to a thickness of approximately 5mm. Using a gingerbread man cookie cutter press out the cookies. Place on a greased baking tray and cook in a pre heated oven set at 190C. Bake for 10 – 15 minutes until they are golden brown. Allow to cool slightly before transferring the cookies to a cooling rack.

Using the writing icing, paint bones onto the cookies to achieve a skeletal appearance.

PUMPKIN SEED LOAF

Serves 4 – 6 People

Far too often we revert to the supermarket for our bread; indeed the making of bread may seem on the surface to be overly complicated, whereas in fact it is quite the opposite. There is something deeply comforting about baking bread, perhaps it is the kneading, the patience required whilst the dough magically swells all of its own accord. Maybe it is the willpower-shattering, delectable, irresistible smell that permeates every room of the house, that makes a home baked loaf the best thing since sliced bread! Get the kids involved, turn the kitchen into a flour spattered Mortuary of ghoulish things.

Ingredients

- 500 ml of warm water
- 7 g sachet of ready to use dry yeast
- 500 g of strong bread flour
- Handful of dried pumpkin seeds

- Olive oil
- Pinch of salt

Method

In a large mixing bowl place the warm water, add the yeast to the water and stir. Leave for 15 minutes to allow the yeast to activate until it becomes creamy and bubbly.

In another bowl combine the flour and salt into which, pour the yeast mixture. Work the mixture until a firm dough is achieved. Combine the pumpkin seeds slowly into the dough.

Place the dough into a clean bowl (you may oil the inside of the bowl to prevent the dough from sticking) cover with a warm damp cloth and allow to rise for an hour or until the twice its original size.

Once the dough has risen, pre heat the oven to 220C. Shape the dough as you wish and place on a baking tray or a loaf tin. With a sharp knife score thin lines into the top of the loaf. Place the dough into the oven and immediately reduce the heat to 180C and bake for 25 – 30 minutes.

The loaf is ready when golden brown and sounds hollow when tapped on the underside.

Remove from the tray or tin and allow to rest on a baking rack for approximately 45 minutes.

Serve with butter and a range of autumnal chutneys.

CAULDRON KORMA

Serves 4 people

The British have always enjoyed a good curry, ever since the arrival of Indian immigrants to our shores the delightful staple that is Curry is a tradition in its own right. This dish is not particularly autumnal, has no gross or spooky element to it, in our thinking it doesn't need it, it's perfect as it is. The recipe suggestion here is for those who prefer a milder curry, but please, you are not limited to this suggestion, many will prefer the stinging thrill of a hot curry rather than its milder cousins.

This dish is made appropriate for the season by serving it in a cauldron; however one of the authors does have an unhealthy amount of cauldrons in his possession, which may not be the case for you the reader. But, fear not, cauldrons can easily be discovered in car boot sales, or attic sales, markets or new age shops, failing that the majority of garden centres sell plastic planters in the shape of Cauldrons, or the various supermarkets will stock them as trick or treat baskets. Use your imagination, if you can get your hands on a real cauldron the more effective the dish, however do ensure that a cast iron cauldron is cleaned and oiled to prevent contamination from the iron. If you happen across a cauldron that looks good but cannot in any shape or form safely accommodate food, simply place the curry in a suitable bowl and insert into the cauldron.

Ingredients

- 700 g of chicken breast or other meat of your choice
- 300 ml of chicken stock
- 4 tablespoons of sunflower oil
- 2 medium onions
- 2 teaspoons of ground ginger
- 2 teaspoons of garlic powder
- 2 teaspoons of ground turmeric
- 4 teaspoons of curry powder
- 2 cans of coconut cream
- 200 ml of single cream
- 100 ml of fresh yoghurt
- Handful of almond slices and fresh coriander.

Method

Pour some oil into a large saucepan and place over a medium heat, add the onions and cook until slightly golden.

In a small bowl add the ground ginger, garlic, curry powder, turmeric to a little water and stir into a paste. Add to the saucepan with the onions and stir well for at least two minutes.

Dice the chicken breasts and add to the pan until the meat is sealed and cooked.

Pour in the chicken stock and continue to cook for a few minutes until the stock has been incorporated fully, now add the coconut cream, the yoghurt and the single cream.

Turn up the heat until the sauce begins to simmer and leave to simmer gently for approximately twenty minutes stirring occasionally.

Whilst the dish is simmering, toast the almonds. Serve these on top of the Korma with some fresh coriander.

Serve with poppadoms, naan bread, onion bhajis, Riata and mango chutney.

COLCANNON

Serves 6 People

Colcannon is a typically Irish dish traditionally served at Halloween, various objects were inserted into the dish and their discovery would foretell the future. Generally used as a cheap, simple yet fulfilling dish throughout the Celtic nations, it fell out of use after the second world war, but is making a resurgence with the revival of old fashioned Halloween traditions. It's a delightfully easy dish to prepare and tastes wonderful; we suggest that you hide coins in the dish real or chocolate for your guests to discover. Foil wrapped chocolate coins are a safe alternative to currency, but bear in mind that they will slightly soften under the heat of the Colcannon. It is said that those who find a coin will be assured of a luck filled year.

Ingredients

- 6 large potatoes
- 1 large Savoy cabbage
- 250 ml of single cream
- 100 g of butter
- Salt
- Coins

Method

Fill a large saucepan with water and a good pinch of salt, place over a high heat and bring to the boil. Peel the potatoes and chop into quarters, drop them into the pool of boiling water reduce the heat and simmer for approximately 20 minutes.

Bring another saucepan of water and a good pinch of salt to the boil. Slice the Savoy cabbage into strips and drop them into the water, simmer for 15 minutes.

When the potatoes are cooked thoroughly remove from the heat and drain in a colander for a few minutes, place back into the saucepan, add the cream and some butter and mash together until smooth.

Drain the cabbage and add to the potato mix.

To serve, place in a bowl or shallow dish, make a little hollow in the top whilst in a small pan melt the remaining butter, pour the melted butter into the well. Lastly push the coins into the mash.

An alternative method of Colcannon is to sauté the cabbage in hot melted butter with the addition of some bacon pieces; add this concoction to the mash mixture.

SWEDE & PUMPKIN SOUP

Serves 4 – 6

This is the perfect blend of autumnal flavours, this simple, easy to make soup is warming, hearty and filling, served in a carved out Swede it makes a perfect lunchtime dish for a cold, windy October day. We have combined the subtle flavour of pumpkin with the delicious, earthy taste of Swede; butternut squash adds autumn hues to the soup.

Ingredients

- 1 large white onion
- 1 whole Swede
- Quarter of a medium sized pumpkin
- Half a large butternut squash
- 2 carrots

- Chicken or vegetable stock cube
- 150 ml of single cream
- 1 garlic clove
- 3 tablespoons of Olive oil

Method

Chop the onion into small chunks and crush the garlic clove, in a large saucepan heat the Olive oil and add the onion and garlic, fry until transparent.

Peel and dice the Swede, pumpkin and butternut squash and carrots and add to the saucepan. Boil the kettle and make up 500 ml's of stock using the stock cube, add to the vegetables and season with salt and pepper.

Allow to simmer until all the vegetables are soft and pulpy, pour in the single cream and blend the soup to your desired consistency. Serve in warmed bowls or in hollowed Swedes with toasted bread.

NAPPY PATTY

Serves 2 – 4 people

They say a picture can convey a thousand words, and no doubt the above photograph will invoke several words, "Gross" and its derivatives perhaps being the most common! But, this is Halloween and all the bets are off, rules have been suspended for 3 fabulous nights, so why night go hell for leather and shock the pants off your guests! This dish is guaranteed to pack a punch, will definitely turn a few stomachs whilst oddly being wonderfully delicious. Get the camera ready to capture the bemused and shocked look on your guest's faces.

Ingredients

- Nappies/Diapers
- A jar of Hazelnut chocolate spread
- 1 small tin of prepared sweet-corn
- Pre purchased Pate (Dark)
- Bread for toasting

Method

Toast some bread and cut into squares that will fit snugly into the bottom part of an open nappy. Smear a good portion of Pate onto the toast.

On the topmost section of the nappy smear the chocolate spread. Don't be meek at this point, go for it, make it look as disgusting as humanly possible, for added 'grossness' add a couple of sweet-corn pieces to the chocolate spread.

Close the nappy carefully so that it resembles a "full" nappy waiting to be disposed of and place at each dinner setting. Ensure the nappies open-end face your guests so that upon opening the nappy they are immediately faced with its hideous contents.

Serve with strips of toast and plastic children's cutlery.

TOFFEE APPLES

Makes 6 – 8 toffee apples

No Halloween book would be complete without the humble toffee apple, they are the ultimate sweet comfort food of the season and a firm Halloween favourite. Although we present here the red toffee variety they can be made in any colour you like.

If you have children in the kitchen do be aware that hot sugar is very dangerous and can cause severe burns, please take precautions if kids are present and do not allow them to stir or touch the hot sugar mixture.

Ingredients

- 2 cups of sugar (brown or white)
- 1 cup of water
- 1 tablespoon of cider vinegar
- 1 tablespoon of red food colouring
- Lemon juice

Method

Begin by carving faces into the apples, these will only be subtly visible through the sugar coating but none the less add a pretty Halloween twist. To prevent the carved areas from turning brown moisten them with a little lemon juice.

In a large heavy based saucepan place the sugar, water and cider vinegar.

Bring the mixture to a rapid boil whilst stirring continuously, add the food colouring a little at a time and continue mixing until the mixture resembles a thick syrup.

To check that the mixture is ready remove a little with a metal spoon and drop into a glass of cold water, if ready the toffee will immediately harden upon contact with the water.

Turn the heat down, impale the apples with sticks, we find that twigs from the garden or park washed and slightly sharpened on one end provide an effective finish. Dip each apple carefully into the toffee mixture ensuring that all parts of the apple are covered.

Place 'stick up' on a greased baking tray or onto waxed paper and allow to set.

DRINKS AND COCKTAILS

What is food without the company of a good drink, with all this eating a healthy thirst is bound to result, and we have just the cure. Halloween cocktails to slay a frightful thirst, although take heed of wearing high heels if you have consumed a few too many of the following suggestions. The majority contain a fair amount of alcohol which, by all means, can be omitted, but what fun would that be? Do be sensible; as we cannot be held responsible for you taking out every herbaceous border in your neighbourhood by diving into them. However tasty, we can assure you that given a few glasses of the following, you will lose the use of your legs. Bodily functions may be somewhat frazzled as a result of over consumption, but hey-ho, one can always have ones stomach pumped!

HOBGOBLIN BEER

The Unofficial Beer of Halloween

When it comes to a long refreshing drink at Halloween nothing quenches a thirsty Home Haunter better than a Hobgoblin Beer! Lovingly created by our friends at the Wychwood Brewery this "Unofficial Beer" is in our eyes "THE Official Beer of Halloween".

"Traditionally craft brewed with chocolate and crystal malts and a blend of Styrian, Goldings and Fuggles hops to produce a full-bodied ruby beer that delivers a delicious chocolate toffee malt flavour, balanced with a rounded moderate bitterness and an overall fruity, mischievous character." (Jeff Drew, Wychwood Brewery, Head Brewer)

Hobgoblin is the perfect beer to drink with meat stews and steak and ales pies (see food recipe section) sausages and mash, burgers and BBQ; roasts; and char-grilled vegetables.

Ingredients

• 500 ml bottle of Hobgoblin

Serve chilled in a large glass and enjoy.

ZOMBIES BRAINS

Guaranteed to get any party started, a quick shot of brains to tickle the senses and perhaps cause the odd heaving or two! This quirky little cocktail looks quite revolting, and the longer it is left standing the thicker the brains become, which can make their consumption rather a task.

Dare your guests take on the Zombies Brains? Find out who amongst your party spits or swallows!

Ingredients

- 2 parts peach flavoured Schnapps
- 1 part Irish cream liqueur
- Dash of Grenadine syrup

Into a suitable shot glass pour out two measures of the peach Schnapps, then carefully and slowly add the Irish cream, this needs to float just under the surface of the Schnapps for the full effect. Slowly pour in a good dash of grenadine for a perfect bloodied appearance. The colours will separate and the Irish cream will react to the Schnapps causing it to congeal.

JACK O LANTERN CIDER

This is a simple, eye catching drink and will look great on Halloween night. Cider drinkers will enjoy the fact that their favourite beverage has not been tampered with, just given a little festive edge.

Ingredients

- Red apples
- English Cider
- Ice

Carve Jack O Lantern style faces into the apples and drop into the bottom of a clear pint glass.

Half fill the glass with ice and slowly pour the cider to the rim of the glass.

Add another slice of apple to garnish.

VAMPIRES KISS

Lose yourself in this indulgent bitter-sweet long drink that entices the senses. The sweetness of cranberry cuts through the bitterness of the coffee liqueur, and its deep, blood red tones would entice any vampire to its intoxicating delights.

Ingredients

- 2 parts Coffee based liqueur
- Cranberry juice
- Ice
- Lime

Pour 2 measures of the coffee based liqueur into a tall glass. Fill with ice and top with cranberry juice and mix. Add a slice of lime to decorate.

GLOWING EYE

This delectable, reliable cocktail is based on the premise that was explored in the previous chapter; UV lights react with tonic water. Wherever UV lights are present these cocktails will glow with a supernatural quality.

Ingredients

- 2 parts Vodka (chilled)
- Tonic water (chilled)
- Fresh lychee's

Pour the vodka and tonic into an iced cocktail shaker and shake the living daylights out of it. Pour into a cocktail glass. Slice the lychee and squeeze the fruit, the pip will give the effect of a pupil, drop into the cocktail, switch on the UV lights and serve.

SPOOK JUICE

This wicked little number will have your guest's tongues slapping their brains out; this cocktail contains more spirits than a haunted house!

Ingredients

- 2 parts apple Vodka
- 2 parts blue Curacao

- 2 parts peach Schnapps
- 1 part lemonade
- Grated apple

Add the apple Vodka, blue Curacao, peach schnapps to a generous glass and stir whilst adding the ice. Top up with the lemonade and stir again. Decorate with grated apple for a deliciously disgusting looking garnish.

SLAUGHTERED ON THE BEACH

There will be no sex on our beaches, we're British! Instead, we get slaughtered on our beaches, particularly at Halloween. Looks pretty, tastes amazing and is extremely moreish, but be careful, looks can be deceiving, too many of these and you will indeed be "Slaughtered"!

Ingredients

- 2 parts Vodka
- 1 part peach Schnapps
- 3 parts cranberry juice
- 3 parts orange juice,
- Splash of Grenadine

Combine the Vodka, peach Schnapps, cranberry juice and orange juice into a large glass and stir.

Fill with ice and gently pour a little grenadine over the ice to create a blood effect.

Serve with a dash of lime and a slice to garnish.

THE HALLOWEEN HEDGEROW

Festive Free Fare

From left to right: A jar of Rowanberry jelly, a jar of Hawthorn berry jelly, a decorative decanter of damson brandy, a noose chokes the neck of a bottle of finest Elderberry vodka. A tall bottle of Sloe Gin begs to be consumed, whilst glasses of Blackberry vodka, Sloe brandy and Elderberry brandy wait to be sipped. A small plate of congealed Bramble blood jelly commands the fore.

Remarkably a whole range of goodies can be harvested from the Hedgerows to compliment the Halloween feast, the range of colours and flavours offer a diverse selection of delectable delights. And the best part of it all – it's practically free! "Hedging" as the craft is called in Britain, has seen a decline over the years, and yet a steady increase of expensive products manufactured from the Hedges glut the market. One can purchase a bottle of sloe gin for a hideous amount of money, yet it can be made for a fraction of the cost, its deep, arterial, bloody colour is a perfect combination for a Halloween dinner party.

The festive period is perfectly placed for the time of harvest; the nation's hedgerows are alive with ripe fruits and berries, begging to be used. Why should the birds have them all? There is plenty to go around.

For the cost of some basic, cheap alcohol and some sugar, you can create amazing, flavourful products in your own kitchen. Whether you live in a town or city or in the countryside, there will be a selection of hedgerow fruits not too far from you. Here follows some simple ideas for making the most of the Halloween Hedgerows.

HOME-MADE HALLOWEEN LIQUEUR'S

Imagine a shelf or cupboard stacked with mysterious bottles of pure autumnal elixirs. Deliciously dark and full bodied liqueurs can be created with the least effort and will keep for several years in a cool dark space. They are the perfect accompaniment to end a meal, or to simply sink back into a comfy sofa before a roaring fire, and taking the weight off your haunted feet, whilst sipping deliciously intoxicating hedgerow creations. Delight your guests with your own alcoholic products, share your bounty at parties or decant into decorative bottles and give as Halloween gifts.

The creating of Halloween liqueurs is based on the simple combination of alcohol, sugar, fruits or berries, for best results use, **Vodka, Gin** or **Brandy**.

The method is simple: Into a large container e.g. a Kilner Jar, place the following components:

- 1 pound of fruit or berries
- 1 pound of sugar
- 1 pint of alcohol

A handy tip to recalling the ingredient amount is to simply chant:
"A Pound. A Pound. A Pint!"
Layer the ingredients into the jar, firmly close the lid and then shake well to combine. Shake the container twice a day, morning and night for between 4 – 6 weeks. The longer the fruits remain in the jar

the more syrupy the final result. When it comes to time, less is more. The concoction is ready when all the sugar has dissolved. Strain the fruit bulk from the liquid and bottle. Keep in a dark cool place.

Some of Britain's best Hedgerow fruits and berries are suggested as follows:

- **Blackberries – Bramble** – The deep purple/black shades of the humble bramble berry make perfectly sweet, tangy Blackberry **Vodka**. Blackberries can be found all over the British Isles, in gardens, woodlands, hedgerows, parks and wastelands, this hardy creature is abundant and the berries burst into ripeness from late September through to October's end. Bear in mind that it is believed that Blackberries are "Kissed by the fairies" after Halloween and should not be picked.

- **Damsons** – Available late summer into early autumn, the deliciously sweet Damson blends perfectly with **Brandy** and with **Gin**, its strong flavours tend to overpower **Vodka**. Damsons can be found on the edges of woodlands in tall shrub like trees.

- **Elderberry** – The beautiful Elder tree is a native of northern Europe; fragrant pale cream flowers decorate the trees in early summer and make excellent cordials and sparkling wines. The elder was considered a sacred tree and it was believed that a person would be cursed if they were to cut it. In late autumn the Elder bursts forth with ripe berries. These small berries can be easily collected, taken from the stalk by passing them through the prongs of a fork and steeped in **Vodka**; the base flavour of **Gin** is too powerful for the berries to compete.

- **Sloeberry** – The sloe berries are the fruits of the Blackthorn tree, a prolific tree that can be found throughout Britain. The sloes are small plum shaped berries, blue/black in colour and often coated in a white, yeasty residue; they are practically inedible whilst raw, owing to their tartness. However when combined with **Gin** they are completely transformed, this famous mixture of sloes and the juniper rich flavours of **Gin** has been a firm favourite in Britain for centuries. But don't just limit them to **Gin**; they also work perfectly well with **Brandy** and **Vodka**.

Serve the liqueurs as aperitifs or with coffee, for a long drink they can be mixed with ice and tonic water.

HOME –MADE HALLOWEEN BLOOD JELLIES

Hedgerow fruits and berries combined with pectin from apples and boiled vigorously, strained and sweetened create perfect Halloween jellies. Not only are they delicious served on warm toast but also make ideal companions for cheese and meat and just happen to look like congealed blood! They can be melted into gravies to add further depths of flavour, or simply served in small dishes for folk to dip into as they fancy. In pretty, decorative jars they make lovely party favours or gifts.

The following cooking method is ideal for Blackberries, Elderberries, Hawthorn berries, Rowanberries and Sloe-berries. Basic ingredients are:

- 3 pounds of Berries
- 2.2 pounds of apples – this provides the pectin needed for setting and will not flavour the jelly
- Enough water to cover the fruit
- Sugar

To prepare a jelly, remove the berries from their stalks and wash. Place in a heavy saucepan with enough water to barely cover the fruit. Slowly bring the mixture to a boil and simmer for approximately 30 minutes or until all the fruits are soft. Allow to cool slightly and then strain through a muslin bag overnight. Take the remaining liquid and place into a clean pan, add 1 pound of sugar for every 1 pint (600ml) of liquid. Heat gently until the sugar has completely dissolved and boil until setting point is achieved.

To check the setting point, drop a small amount of the jelly onto a cold, refrigerated plate and run your finger through the jelly; if set the mixture will wrinkle and appear congealed. Pour the hot liquid into warm jars and seal.

GAMES AND DIVINATION
Fun and Frolics

If at midnight with pumpkin light,
You steal to your room unseen,
In the mirror appears the face,
Of your lover true, on Halloween
(Early 20th century postcard)

Games are an ancient form of simple entertainment; they hearken back to the old days when we were responsible for creating our own fun. It is only in recent decades that we have been able to immerse ourselves in products created for us by the entertainment industry, but every now and then going back to the old fashioned fun-filled methods are incredibly amusing.

Halloween is renowned for a time of games and frolics, and although many of them are designed with children in mind, there is absolutely no reason why they cannot be performed by adults. In fact we encourage the adults out there to throw themselves into the spirit of the season, and act your shoe size not your age. After all it is Halloween and all normal rules are suspended for this one, crazy night.

What follows is a smattering of games for kids or adults, and following them, for novelty value, we have included some of the old, traditional forms of games. These in a sense are divinatory games, in other words they act as forms of divination and allegedly tap into the bank of supernatural power available to us on Halloween night. Many of them are too old to date; some come from the Victorian era when magic and superstition were a part of life, when séances and mediums would frequent parties and events. The ones included here are quite harmless, so worry not; no demons will intrude upon you, but then again who knows!

Pumpkin Fettling

This oddly bizarre, verging on the almost dangerous and foolhardy originates from the south of England and continuous to be a popular Halloween practise in the county of Dorset. It's a little crazy, but quite a lot of fun and very simple to create. In a manner it mimics the old pub game of Bar Billiards, which is a miniature version of ten pin bowling. Pumpkin Fettling is a cross between these two games involving a large pumpkin and 8 very nervous participants!

For this game you will need:

- 8 volunteers, however reluctant!
- 8 posts for the volunteers to stand upon, logs generally work well
- 1 large pumpkin
- Approx 20 feet of thin rope
- A blindfold

Oh and not forgetting the Fettler itself, i.e. the person lobbing the Pumpkin at the volunteers!

Method:

Cut a hole in the top and bottom of the pumpkin, and using a long rod or stick thread the rope through the body of the pumpkin and out the bottom end. Tie a large knot at the bottom end of the rope to secure it firmly to the pumpkin. Hang the pumpkin from a beam, a branch or other device that will allow good long swingage!

Place the logs or pedestals in a staggered arrangement approximately 10 feet away from the hanging pumpkin. The Fettler must then be blindfolded and guided to the hanging pumpkin. The Fettler then takes the pumpkin and similar to bowling throws it towards his skittles, in this case a bunch of anxious folk probably not looking their best by this point in dodgy fancy dress! The purpose of the game; well I don't suppose there is one actually, for it will take on a sadistic life of its own! But ultimately, the last person standing is declared the winner.

Cautiously, and perhaps wisely, do remember that the pumpkin is somewhat heavy and can cause damage to soft, let's just say delicate parts of the human anatomy! So aim to hit the volunteers somewhere in the mid section! Generally, the game will be dependent on the amount of space that you have, an indoor barn space for instance would be perfect, as would a large garden with a good sized tree. Your mother's living room may not be a good idea, as the pumpkin once fettled is alas an unstoppable force oddly attracted to expensive ornaments! The rules are fluid, the game adaptable, so go on, be inventive, after all it is Halloween!

Donut Face

The aim of this game is painfully simple. Purchase several donuts, of the ringed variety preferably sugared, and just for luck cover them in even more sugar! Using thin twine or string, hang the donuts from a suitable device, we find the washing line to be perfect and prevents donut being walked into the carpet!

Participants are suitable restrained, hands tied behind their backs and led to the line of donuts, the aim - the first person to consume their donut entirely without licking their lips!

Botulism Bet's Chocolate Surprise

This bizarre game can be as pleasant or unpleasant as its creator, so participants beware! The game has no aim as such but does present a rather amusing party piece.

Gather as many edible foodstuffs as you can, each item should be no bigger than a quarter of an inch or so. Let only your imagination restrict you, so gather cut up strawberries, a little pumpkin perhaps, some banana, blueberries, cheese, cut ham, garlic, tuna, we have even heard of someone using dog food!! Nasty! Place all the items on a tray covered in waxed or greaseproof paper. In a double boiler, i.e. a heavy glass bowl over a pan of boiling water (do not allow the pan to boil dry) melt some chocolate, any chocolate will do. When sufficiently melted and using a metal spoon, cover the food items in a chocolaty coating! There will come a point where even you will not remember what lies beneath the chocolate. Allow to set firmly in the refrigerator then place in a bowl or a suitable platter, present to your guests and delight in the anxiety, pleasure and sheer disgust that may follow!

Apple Bobbing

Perhaps the most traditional game most relevant to Halloween, it is incredibly simple yet immensely amusing. The house proud should perhaps take heed and ensure the game is performed outdoors, otherwise we suggest a large tarpaulin or other form of plastic sheeting to be placed on the floor. A large amount of water can be displaced during play, and one does not want the living room transformed into a scene from Waterworld!

For this game the little equipment you will need is as follows:

- A large container – a large plastic bucket, or garden container is perhaps the easiest.
- Plastic sheeting – tarpaulin
- Apples
- Water

Fill the container to within about 6 inches of the rim with water, a tip here is to use warm water, or straight cold water from the tap with a few kettles of hot water added to remove the chill. The last thing you need is hypothermic guests on your hands! Drop in as much apples as can float on the surface of the water. The amount of participants will be dictated by the size of the vessel used. Players kneel beside the container; their hands should be loosely tied behind their backs.

The aim is to retrieve as many apples as possible by use of the teeth alone. The winner is he or she who manages to grab the most apples.

Tangled Spiders

This game will have you rolling around in laughter, kids and adults will love it equally. May we suggest, for adults, that it is best played after partaking of a few cocktails from the recipe section!

The larger the number of players the better and messier the game becomes!

All that is required is some balls of wool, no more than 5 balls in total. "Pound shops" and discount stores will have some in stock, any type will do.

All players should stand in a circle; give the balls of wool to a number of people in the circle, equally dispersed. These players should tie the loose end of the wool around their waists and then throw the ball to the opposite side of the circle. The person who catches the wool should also tie it around their waist, and then throw the ball of wool back across the circle. As more and more balls fly across the circle and more and more players become 'tied up' a huge spider's web will emerge in the centre of the circle.

The game has no actual aim other than to create a web. Some spooky background music and plenty of encouragement from the onlookers will ensure a fun filled 10 minutes or so.

Loo-Roll Mummies

A crazy game, fun for kids and adults alike! For this game you will require some willing volunteers and several rolls of loo paper! The aim of the game is simple, to create an Egyptian Mummy with toilet paper, inelegantly wrapped around a player.

Split the players into teams of 3 people, one is be to the mummy and the remaining players will be the wrappers. Give the wrappers a roll of paper each.

At a signal, the wrappers begin enveloping the victim in loo paper; do ensure that the mouth and nose remain free of paper! If the paper breaks then simply tuck it in and keep going. The winning team is the one which completes the task first.

ANCIENT GAMES

Hallowed Stones

The following is an old game from Celtic times.

On Hallowmas eve when the bonfires are lit, each member of the community should take a single white stone. Upon the face of the stone a symbol must be etched that identifies the stone to its owner. The stones must then be cast into the flames. Upon dawn of the morrow, each person seeks to find his or her own stone amongst the cold embers and ashes. Those who find their stones are deemed fortunate and their year will pass with no trouble. To he or she who does not find their stone, alas they will suffer a dreadful year and much misfortune.

Peel the Future

At the stroke of midnight on All Hallows eve, take into your chamber the finest apple available to thee. And there in secret peel the apple so that the peel is removed in one piece. Then stand before a window and with much thought cast the peel over thy left shoulder. Henceforth, turn about and study the shape and pattern by which the peel has fallen. If the hallowed spirits do smile upon you, the initial of thy future love will be formed from the apple skin.

The Apple and the Mirror

Near the hour of midnight on All Hallows eve, secret yourself away to the privacy of a room in which there is a mirror. Take with you a single candle and a fine apple. The candle should be lit and placed in front of the mirror. Now with a sharp knife cut the apple into nine segments, 8 of which you should consume yourself whilst your back is to the mirror, just before the clock strikes 12. As soon as the chime of midnight is heard, cast the 9th segment over your left shoulder so that it strikes the mirror, at this point make haste and turn swiftly about. You will catch a glimpse of your future love in the looking glass.

A variation of this rite is performed whilst looking into the mirror; eat an apple from your left hand whilst brushing your hair with your opposite hand. The rite should be performed at midnight and as the latter, your lover will appear to you in the looking glass.

Shell's of the heart

Write on the shells of two walnuts the names,
Of two of your sweethearts and throw in the flames,
The shell that cracks the first is your lover's name,
Be good to him and date he'll proclaim.
(Early 20th century Halloween postcard)

Falling love

Near Midnight on All Hallows Eve, a man should take to his bed chamber a clean glass filled with water. Upon this water he should float a small piece of wood. If the spirits are in agreement, the man will dream of falling from a bridge into a pool of water. Whosoever appears within the dream to rescue him shall be his true love.

The String Eaters

When two unmarried maidens seek to know who shall marry the first, then they should take a piece of string or thread of fair length and tie at its middle a raisin. The ends of the string should then be taken in their mouths. So, standing some feet apart the maidens face each other, the string should now be taught, and the raisin held fast in its middle.

Upon a given signal the maidens chew at the string, moving closer and closer to the raisin. Whosoever takes the raisin first shall marry.

The Dishes of Destiny

As the sun sets on Hallows eve, take 3 of the finest bowls in the house. The fairest tablecloth should adorn the table in preparation for this rite. Now into the first bowl pour good clean water, whilst into the second pour in dirty water, the third bowl shall remain empty. She who seeks the future should now be led blindfolded into the room in which the bowls are arranged, and placed before them. The woman is encouraged to reach out with her left hand in the direction of the bowls. If she touches the bowl which contains the clean water, she will marry a young, attractive man. If it be the dirty water which she touches first, then she shall marry instead an older man, perhaps a widower, but a man who is also kind and fair. However if she touches the empty bowl then she shall remain unmarried for the duration of the year.

TALES OF TERROR

Tis the night – the night,
Of the grave's delight,
And the warlocks are at their play;
Ye think that without
Without the wild winds shout,
But no, it is they- it is they.
(Arthur Cleveland Coxe 1818 - 1896)

Halloween naturally accentuates the terrifying and downright scary, tales of terror, superstition, ghouls and witches fit perfectly into the seasonal quality of Halloween. With dark nights and shadows creeping at your door, the flicker of candlelight and the very threat of the dead sneaking about, just waiting to scare the life out of you, all adds to the sense of fun filled terror. However desensitised we have become owing to the increasingly shock filled movies that most of us love and adore; nothing quite beats the amazing ability of our own imagination.

From the dawn of time, mankind has gathered as a community, around the warming glow of a fire, to tell tales of achievements, victory, moral codes and ethics. All of these tied in wonderfully into the oral tradition, the telling of tales. Storytelling has been a vital part of every civilisation on the planet, and their effectiveness relies on a simple, powerful device; the human imagination.

Urban legends, you know the tale that is really true and actually happened to a friend of a friend of mine! We have all heard them and generally we all love them, they are simultaneously horrifying and entertaining. Being, short, straightforward yet crammed to the brim with images that our imaginations invoke, they are perfect Halloween companions. Of course the tales are not in any shape or form true, they are a clever invention which takes elements of storytelling, remove any message of history or metaphor and they exist simply to terrify.

You may already be familiar with the offering of tales in this section, they don't belong to any particular country or place, they are adaptable and applicable to anywhere. So grab one that sends chills up your spine, place it in your community, dim the lights, hush the volume of your voice, and frighten the hell out of your listeners. But remember to ensure that your audience knows that the tale is true and actually happened to someone you knew, keep the spirit of the Urban – Campfire legend alive!

The Haunted Motel

Ken had been driving for what seemed like an age, it was late, the weather was terrible, he was cold, tired and desperately wanting to stop and rest. Along the road he happened across a lonely motel, just your typical run of the mill Motel that everybody passes on the motorway but pays little attention to. To Ken it was a godsend and meant a break from the monotony of endless driving. He decided to stop and rest and to continue his journey the following day. Hoping that they had a room available he parked his car, stretched his tired legs and entered the reception area.

The manager informed him that there were only two rooms left, and that they were next door to each other, however, one of them was renowned for being haunted, whilst the other was not. Ken wasn't quite sure what to make of this unexpected bit of information, and although not a superstitious kind of man, he decided not to tempt fate and take the non-haunted room.

By the time he had retrieved his overnight bag from the car, got into his room, locked the door, staggered to the mercy of a hot shower and tumbled into bed, he had forgotten what the manager had said. Within minutes Ken was fast asleep.

He noticed that it was 3am when he woke up, he couldn't be sure what had stirred him from his sleep, but something had. In the dark room only the dim green glow of the clock radio shone in the darkness, except for a bright beam of light that seemed to be coming from a small hole in the wall above the bed. He got to his knees and peered through the hole, which to his surprise looked directly into the room next door. The Haunted room next door seemed perfectly ordinary, he could see a woman in a white nightgown standing in the room with her back to him; he felt a little awkward spying on her and took back to his bed. Within minutes he was asleep again.

An hour later he awoke once more, although this time no light emitted from the hole in the wall, his curiosity got the better of him and he rose to his knees to take a peek. His eyes strained to see into the room next door, but he could see nothing other than the colour red, no furniture, no room, jut a red dim glow. Perplexed, he shrugged it off and wrapped himself back under the sheets.

The next morning, much refreshed and eager to carry on his journey, he gathered his things and checked out. The manager enquired if he slept ok, and asked "Did you see the ghost of the girl next door?"

To which Ken replied "Well, there is a hole in the wall, and I couldn't help but look and saw a pretty girl next door, she had her back to me, but she didn't look like a ghost at all!"

The manager said, "Ah, you didn't see her eyes then did you? They are blood red."

Roomates

Katie and Ellen shared a house, they had been best of friends since college and figured that until they found their situations changed they were better off sharing a home together. Ellen had been suffering with a bad cold for the last few days, it had taken its toll and after persevering for three days, she decided to stay off work and take to her bed.

Katie had plans with her boyfriend that Friday night, but felt guilty leaving Ellen alone at home, however Ellen informed her that she wasn't a child and would be fine. "Go out!" She said. "Enjoy yourself, I'll be fine, if you stay with Mike, that's cool too, I'll catch you later or tomorrow. Go!"

Reluctantly Katie relented and got herself ready for her night out. Once out she forgot all about poor Ellen home alone with a cold. Her boyfriend Mike tried convincing her to stay at his that night, claiming that there was nothing that she could actually do for Ellen and that all she needed was rest. Eventually Katie agreed, but remarked that she wanted to go home first, check on Ellen and get some fresh clothes so she could go straight to work from Mikes in the morning.

The house was in darkness when she arrived, Mike waited for her in the car. Quietly she crept up the stairs, avoiding the creaking stair half way up. Ellen's bedroom door was slightly ajar, and she could hear her soft breathing, although she could tell the cold had gone to her chest by the slight crackling in her snoring. She retrieved some clothing from her own room, and realised that her overnight bag was in Ellen's room after her friend had borrowed it last week.

Silently she opened the door, and knowing where the bag was, reached in without switching on the lights and felt for the bag. She found it just to the right of the open door. Quietly she pulled the door almost shut and retreated.

The following day she decided to head home during her lunch break to check on Ellen. She was surprised to see a police cordon in her street, uniformed officers stood guard, and she could see the distinctive white overalls of a forensic team going in and out of her house! She approached a police officer and explained that she lived there, and asked what was going on. A senior detective was called to speak to her.

"Were you not home last night Miss?" He asked.

"No, but I did come by to get some stuff, Ellen was asleep, what's going on?"

The detective asked her to follow him into the house. He wanted her to see something that she may be able to explain. Ellen's room was disarrayed and the bed covered in fresh blood stains, spatters of which decorated the walls like a bizarre mural. The detective informed her that her friend had been murdered during the night. As he spoke he moved to the wall behind the bed and removed a large sheet of plastic that hung there.

"Can you explain this Miss?" He asked and pointed to the wall, upon which was inscribed in Ellen's own blood the words –

"Aren't you glad you didn't turn on the lights?"

In the Same Room

It had been snowing hard for the past 2 days; a heavy white, pristine blanket lay over the land. Mandy was home alone, her parents had braved the snow and ventured out to a dinner party. Mandy resigned herself to curl up on the sofa under a warm blanket to watch the TV. Beyond the large patio doors, in front of which stood the TV, the garden glowed with a bluish light, reflecting the crisp snow. It was a perfect winter scene.

As the night drew on and midnight approached, Mandy's parents had yet to return, her blood turned cold when she noticed a man standing outside the window just behind the TV. He stood perfectly still his head tilted down as if he was staring at the ground beneath his feet.

Mandy froze to the sofa, quickly she threw the blanket over her head, thankfully her mobile phone was right beside her. She dialled the police and explained that someone was stalking the house and that she was terribly afraid. The police controller told her that a patrol car was in her street and that the officers would be there in a couple of minutes. Mandy breathed a sigh of relief.

Two minutes passed, slowly Mandy emerged from beneath the blanket, to her relief the man had gone, and that very moment the doorbell rang. The presence of the police instantly put her at ease. They checked outside the patio doors and throughout the garden, but oddly not a single footprint was found in the freshly fallen snow. Mandy, perplexed, was aware that the officers were beginning to think she had simply dreamt the whole thing, when suddenly one of the officers froze in mid sentence.

He stood behind the sofa upon which Mandy had been seated when she saw the strange man. Mandy noticed his reaction; he seemed to be staring down at the floor behind the sofa. She knelt onto the sofa and leaned over its back to see what the matter was. Her blood turned to ice in her veins when she saw wet dirty footprints on the carpet behind the sofa. The man had not been outside the window at all, it was his reflection she saw, he had been in the same room!

In The Corner

Tracy had been asked to babysit for a new family; she had a good reputation and found herself in an enormous house in a nice section of town. The kids were well behaved, and the father explained that once she had the kids settled that she was welcome to help herself to anything she wanted. She was given a room in a part of the house close to the children's bedrooms in which to stay the night.

The kids gave her no trouble and they were soon sound asleep. Tracy made herself some food and retired to the comfortable room that the owners had provided for her. She lay sprawled on the bed watching late night television, but a clown statue in the corner of the room kept catching her eye. It started making her feel uneasy, and a little frightened. Although innocent looking, she accused herself of being overdramatic, but she was certain its eyes were watching her intensely.

An hour or so later, she was beginning to get a little freaked out so she decided to call the owner.

"Would you mind if I changed rooms?" She asked. "I know it's a little stupid of me, but I am getting really freaked out by the clown statue in the corner!"

"Get the kids, go next door and call the police, right now!" The owner exclaimed.

Tracy felt her blood run cold as panic froze her to the core. Not daring to look at the clown she rushed from the room, woke the children and marched them next door, before calling the police.

The police arrived at the same time as the owner. "What's going on?" asked Tracy.

"We don't have a clown statue!" He replied.

It transpires that a psychopathic midget, dressed as a clown had escaped from the local mental institution and was hiding out in the house. When the babysitter had entered the room, he froze in the corner assuming she would believe him to be a toy.

Mothers Milk

Bob had owned the local shop all his life, he didn't remember a time that it wasn't a part of his life. The village had turned into a small town during those years. Bob was a kind, gentle man, loved and respected by his customers; the shop grew into the heart of the community.

It wasn't often that strangers came into the shop, except during the busy summer months when folk would venture on hikes into the surrounding mountains. He was curious to note a woman he had not seen before enter the shop and walk directly to the refrigerated cabinet. Ho noticed her mostly because she seemed bedraggled and anxious. She removed two milk cartons from the fridge, and although he voiced a greeting, she paid him no heed. Instead she turned about and promptly walked out of the shop without paying.

He may have ventured after her had other customers not come in at that very moment, he thought he should call the police or chase after her, but something about her, the desperation in her eyes told him to ignore it.

She was back the next day, he was serving an old customer when he noticed her move swiftly to the fridge, he gestured to his customer who also noticed her remove a milk carton and swiftly leave the shop. She offered neither a penny nor an acknowledgment. Her demeanour was much more disturbed this time; she seemed on the edge of distress. Once again Bob shrugged it off, she must be desperate, and maybe he could offer her a part time job if she came in again, or just try and speak to her.

She did come back, the very next morning. And the routine was the same; she took a single carton this time. Bob called after her, but she did not respond. This time, he chased after her, calling to a friend in the shop next door to watch his store for a while. He followed the woman, who oddly seemed to be just a few paces ahead of him however quickly he followed. She led him a good mile before entering the new cemetery on the edge of town. Bob wasn't familiar with this place; it was new and accommodated the dead from several villages in the area. The woman moved swiftly through the cemetery and stopped abruptly at a freshly filled grave. Bob barely believed his eyes when she suddenly vanished, right there before his eyes.

A sound rose to meet his ears, he shook his head in bafflement, it was the muffled cry of a baby that he heard and it seemed to coming from the fresh grave! He quickly called the police on his mobile phone and they arrived in minutes, with the gravedigger in tow. The grave was opened and the coffin removed. Upon opening the coffin, Bob gave out a piercing cry of horror. Inside the grave lay the freshly dead corpse of the woman he had followed, a baby cried loudly between her legs, and there at the foot of the coffin were the cartons of milk stolen from his shop. The woman's ghost had alerted Bob to the fact her baby was still alive.

Ice Cold

Bill couldn't help but notice the girl who stared at him from across the bar. In fact he could hardly believe that she was looking at him at all, and smiling! After all Bill was quite a plain looking man, only in his late twenties, but handsome wasn't a word folk would generally associate with Bill. Women and Bill had never really worked, they weren't that interested in getting to know him.

His heart nearly leapt from his chest when this fine woman, rose from her seat and casually walked over towards him. He looked around, thinking she must be headed for someone else, but no, he was the only guy at that end of the bar.

"Hi!" She said pleasantly, "My name's Kim, are you here alone?"

He could hardly answer, but managed to stutter out words that partially answered her question; she giggled and called the barman over. Within minutes they were chatting and drinking together, Bill was enthralled by the woman. He was sure that she could hear his heart beating like a drum in his chest.

The impossible happened! Well, previously impossible for Bill! She asked him to go upstairs to her hotel room, her hand swept gracefully up his leg, barely passing his groin, her intent was quite clear. Bill felt a stirring in his nether regions that he had not felt in a long time. He took less than a second to answer and followed her up the stairs.

In her luxurious hotel room she retrieved a bottle of champagne from the mini fridge and proceeded to pour a glass each. With a wink she entered the bathroom and only minutes later reappeared in the sexiest lingerie set Bill had ever had the pleasure to view on a woman. He knocked his champagne back in one fell swoop! His eyes must be betraying him, he thought. His lips however really did feel her red, plump lips kissing him with a passion he had never experienced before. His heart threatened to stop under the intensity of it, his head swam crazily and the room vanished into darkness,

It was the cold he felt first, not the warmth of a woman's lips but the icy, sharp cold, even before he opened his eyes, his body shivered uncontrollably. He was confused, totally disorientated when, from beneath the shiver arose the pain, a searing white pain across his side. His eyes opened, sticky and dry; he lay in a bath of water and ice cubes, filled to the brim. A pink tinged stain ran through the water. His breathing shallow and fast increased as his eyes were drawn to the writing on the mirror which adorned the wall at the foot of the bath, a mobile phone sat oddly beneath it.

"You have no kidneys. If you want to live, call 999"

Bill realised that the woman didn't want him after all, just his organs to sell on the black market. Bill never had any luck with women, panic caught him about the neck and a cold, terrible scream rose from his lungs.

Lick

Cassie was used to being left alone, her parents worked night shifts. She was never one to be nervous or anxious alone, but her parents had bought her dog, just for company they said. Cassie loved her dog, which mostly spent the night fast asleep under the bed. Late one night Cassie was awoken to a strange sound, she pricked her ears and listened intently, it was the sound of something dripping. She arose from her bed and staggered sleepily through to the kitchen and firmly turned all the taps shut. She pattered back to her bed, and reached down under the bed to reassure the dog that all was well, she sighed contentedly as the dog licked her hand.

However the dripping sound continued, with annoyance she tried the bathroom and firmly turned the taps shut, back in her bed she reached down under the bed and the dog licked her hand again. She wrapped herself in her duvet and closed her eyes, but the dripping noise continued. She got to her feet and stood quietly, listening carefully, she fathomed that the sound seemed to be coming from her built in wardrobe! Cautiously she approached the tall mirrored doors and slid one open.

Her screams peeled through the house as she was confronted with the sight of her dog, hanging upside down, its throat brutally cut. Behind it on the wooden back of the closet, written in the dogs' blood were the words – "Humans can lick too!"

In the Back Seat

Nicky had been driving for hours, her eyes were dry and uncomfortable, and to make it worse it had started raining. She had no idea how much longer she had to go, the road seemed endless, it didn't help that she was a stranger to these parts. She was beginning to regret driving from London to Scotland, she should have flown.

The rain continued to pelt down against the windscreen; the wipers seemed useless against the downpour. Up ahead she noticed a mini supermarket and decided to pull over and get a drink, the short sprint from the car to the supermarket soaked her to the skin. She rushed into the shop and was relieved to see that they sold fresh, hot coffee. With a few sips of the hot drink inside her, she quickly ventured back to the car and continued her journey.

Twenty minutes later the petrol light came on; she breathed a sigh of relief to see a lonely petrol station just up ahead. A creepy, half witted man rushed out to fill her car with fuel whilst she remained in the car. She handed her credit card to him through the window, and watched him stagger to the office. A moment later he hurtled out asking her to come in as there was a problem with her card. She sighed in annoyance and followed him into the warm office.

As she walked in the attendant slammed the door behind her and bolted it shut. Nicky started shouting at him, demanding to know what the hell he was doing. However the attendant's stutter prevented him from speaking to her properly and her screaming and shouting made it all so much worse.

"Th-thee-thuh-uh, i-i-i-ts-bee-bee-cos!" He tried to explain, but it was no use Nicky was not standing for it, she pushed him hard against the wall, tore her credit card from his hand and rushed for the door. She threw back the bolts slamming her elbows into the attendant's stomach as he tried to apprehend her. She ran to the car and slammed the door, thrashing to get the key into the ignition. Finally the key engaged; the engine burst into life and with screeching tyres Nicky sped off into the darkness.

Behind her on the forecourt the attendant suddenly managed to find his words and screamed into the night "Th-th-THERE's – SOMEONE – IN – THE – BACK – SEAT!"

Nicky didn't hear his cry, neither did she hear the movement of fabric in the back seat, she didn't hear the chill wind of the axe as it slammed into the side of her neck. She didn't hear a thing as her head separated from its body and fell into the foot well, its eyes still blinking, watching the fountain of blood gushing from the neck it was just attached to.

146 . HALLOWEEN

HALLOWEEN TRIVIA

When spirits go riding
And black cats are seen
When the moon laughs in whisper
'Tis near Halloween
(Early 20th century postcard)

- Samhain is Irish Celtic meaning "Summers End" it is not the Druidic god of death.

- Acrophobia is the fear of heights.

- The colour Orange is associated with Halloween because of autumn leaves.

- Achluophobia is the irrational fear of darkness.

- Black is associated with Halloween because of its associations with death and decay.

- Astraphobia is the fear of thunder and or lightning.

- Halloween is a Pagan and Roman Catholic festival.

- Blennophobia is the fear of slime.

- In the USA, Halloween is the second most commercially successful festival. Christmas takes the lead.

- Catotrophobia is the irrational fear of mirrors.

- A Swede was introduced into Scotland from Sweden.

- Coimetrophobia is the irrational fear of cemeteries.

- The apple is sacred to the Roman Goddess Pomona

- Felinophobia is the fear of cats.

- Halloween first arrived in America with Irish immigrants.

- Hadephobia is the irrational fear of Hell.

- The Halloween industry in Britain during 2010 was worth £280 million.

- Haemophobia is the fear of blood.

- Sales of fangs in the UK were up 13% after the release of the first Twilight movie.

- Herpetophobia the fear of reptiles.

- There are no words in the English language that rhyme with the word "Orange".

- Samhainapohobia is an irrational fear of Halloween.

- Turnips, Beets and Mangel Wurzel's were the original Jack O Lanterns.

- Paraskavedekatriaphobia is a fear of the number 13.

- Parker brothers USA make and sell ten different brands of Ouija boards.

- Phasmophobia is the fear of ghosts.

- The word 'Pumpkin' comes from the Greek to mean a large melon.

- Pneumatiphobia is the fear of spirits.

- People wore costumes and masks to disguise themselves from wandering spirits.

- Sciophobia is the fear of shadows.

- The first Halloween card was manufactured in the 1920's.

- Spectrophobia is the fearing of seeing spectres or ghosts.

- In the USA over 91% of children will engage in Trick or Treat.

- Taphophobia is the fear of being buried alive.

- Halloween candy sales in the USA average $2 billion a year.

- Thanatophobia is the fear of death or dying.

- Halloween is one of the world's oldest festivals.

- Wiccaphobia is the fear of witches or witchcraft.

- Halloween is not and never has been "evil".

POST MORTEM

THE FUTURE OF HALLOWEEN

Tis, the night, the night, of ghouls delight,
When cauldrons boil o'er ghostly light,
By Punkie's glow, a Souling we'll go,
To greet the dead who rot below.
Three nights that bring the ancestors near,
Through veils so thin they gather here,
No rules, nor neither slight nor sin,
Shall spoil our joyous Halloween din.
(K. Hughes, 2011)

Anything that has relevance will endure; anything that brings people together will survive. As we have explored in this book Halloween has endured, is enduring and will continue to endure for many centuries to come, perhaps for the entire duration of our species existence. In a sometimes frightful world where terror has such a real and tangible component, it is no great surprise that as a people we turned to its antithesis, the creation of conjectured terror for the sake of entertainment. We have also seen that throughout the practises of Halloween, ancient and modern, there are tendrils of originality that reach back through the dank soil, through land and culture to the dawning of civilisations.

149

We have also explored and described that on a symbolic level; that far exceeds the understanding of children, that their current Halloween rites embody a sacred exchange between the visible and invisible worlds.

We have also attempted to explain the worthiness of the festival, its vitality and importance to us as people of the Celtic and Western world. It is alas, the one remaining indigenously Celtic feast that continues to survive and is celebrated by countless millions of people. We have also seen how the festivals sublime or spiritual significance, does not negate its frivolous or profane aspect, but rather adds a magical quality to it, and neither, we have found, does the frivolous inadvertently affect the sublime. With this in mind we conclude that Halloween is far from being a sacrilegious festival but rather an entity whose sacred origins rise from the dawn of time.

On the other hand we have also borne witness to the evolution of Halloween and its adoption by several cultures. Celebration lies at the heart of our modern Halloween festivities, and the abandonment of conformity, we are practically encouraged to break the rules and let our hair down. And we have done this with gumption and a sense of vigour, reclamation and joy. The overall sense that people have of its past, its origins, is almost irrelevant, ignorance of its history does not and cannot dilute its virility and aliveness.

The beast that we know as Halloween has a life of its own, an image that has been personified by novels and recently movies, where the personification of the festival has literally taken on a life of its own. In 2008 the director Michael Dougherty's movie "Trick r Treat", featured a symbolic anthropomorphic creature called Sam, a seemingly sinister mascot of Halloween. In fact the character seemed also to be the festivals mystical guardian, terrorising those who did not display a lantern, or whom otherwise belittled the season. This concept in itself is not wholly original, but instead seems to draw on a myriad of ancient myths, lore and traditions to create a manifestation of the festival. This and other popular Hollywood productions continuously inspire and inadvertently perpetuate the season.

But what of the future? The obvious increase in Halloween merchandise and products cannot be disputed, and major corporations are cashing in on this surprising bounty. Against all the odds and a worldwide economic recession, Halloween has survived, thanks mostly to its modern position in the entertainment industry. To many this strikes a cold deal at the heart of Samhain, whilst to others it is simply the twenty first century's natural expression of Halloween, like most things in life; balance is needed. Both aspects have their place, both have legitimate claim over the festival. In truth, the sacred and the profane are inseparable. What we can be assured of is that increase it will, in popularity and celebration.

Unlike Christmas with its red coated, jolly mascot at its centre, or Easter with its bunny and associations with the Christian saviour, Halloween stands unique. It is not reliant upon a mascot nor a patron, a saint or a spirit, a god or any other deity to hold it together, to give it substance or connection to a created entity. Instead, as we have seen, it relies upon something else, something more intrinsically human; our need to feel good, to come together in warmth and company. And, perhaps more importantly, our innate fear of death. With these qualities at its heart, Halloween has no need for a mascot to give it credence; it has and always will have – a mind of its own.

The Islands of Britain are undergoing a Halloween revolution, and the future is dark, gloomy and wonderfully sinister! We may not as of 2011, have reached the dizzying heights of expression, enjoyed by our American cousins, but there are significant stirrings amidst Britain's green and pleasant land. Increasingly October brings with it a host of companies, shops and businesses displaying elaborate decorations of the season for the public to observe. This inspires individuals and families to band together, to create events pertinent to that unit or group. Our theme parks abound with gore and frights to titillate their fear-hungry guests, whilst pumpkin farms adorn the British countryside, a sight that is of much amusement to our older generations who have never seen such spectacles.

There is also a sense of reclamation, America has never been under any illusions that Halloween is an import, made relevant and applicable to their culture, the Brit's alas still claim it is nothing other than an import. This sad fact, not only belies a sense of ignorance in our own historic record but also an unwillingness to engage with our past and celebrate it. Things are steadily changing, information is readily available, the people of Britain are slowly realising that the roots of Halloween is wondrously British in origin and should be celebrated as such. This blend of information, education, frivolity and frolic is the reason this book sprang into being.

So, people of Britain, next time you pass a grinning ghost, a plastic severed arm hanging from a bush or the benign, crooked smile of a Punkie lantern. When you see a cauldron burning, or hear the mocking tones of *"Trick or Treat"* being called about the streets, when whispers of the dead reach you from tomb and grave. Smile to yourself, for they are your heritage, they are yours to claim, this season of frights and treats is 'your' season. So; light candles at each window to guide the dead, festoon your garden in glorious gore and serve gargantuan meals of hideous appeal. Adorn your abode with decor fit for the spirits, don your finest mourning attire, put the vodka on ice and celebrate as if your are trying to wake the dead!

The future is dark, foreboding and creepy, the dead chuckle at the attention, and the chiming bells of doom ring out through the cold autumn evenings. Place an ear against an ancient chamber, stop and prick up your ears whilst passing a graveyard, listen intently, and perhaps you will hear – the joyous cackling of the dead awaking to the peeling screams that ring above. After two thousand years, Halloween is coming home.

Quintessentially British, it is indeed a season of treats and frights!

MEET THE AUTHORS

Mark Doody

Where did this fascination for Halloween start with me? It's hard to pin point exactly, but I guess I have to blame my parents. I remember as a small child watching horror movies with my mum and dad. They would always warn me that they could be scary, but being a defiant child I would always put on a face of 'nothing scares me' when actually it bloody well did!!

To make matters worse, whenever a scary part of the film came on; my mum would always cover my eyes, only for me to hear screams of death and torture, leading to a thirst of wanting to see what was going on. I think actually hearing a horror film as a child is much more disturbing than seeing it, it's like reading a book where your imagination can take over and fill in the gaps!

Sundays were always 'video' day in our house. My dad would drive up the road to get fuel on a Sunday and back in those days (VHS, or Betamax had just taken the world by storm) our local petrol station would stock a small selection of films for hire. While dad filled the car with fuel, I would run into the store to view the videos available. Never reading what a film was actually about, I was always drawn to the most sickening and scary front cover, saying "Dad, dad, we have to watch this" as long as it had a monster or blood on the front cover I was sold!

When Halloween came, I can't honestly say that we had parties or celebrated it much, as to be honest it wasn't really the 'thing to do' back in the late seventies especially in the United Kingdom. My parents would always get me a plastic mask, either a vampire or Frankenstein and that would be about it. Bear in mind I was only around seven years old, but Halloween did freak me out a little, especially with the belief that the dead would walk about that evening. I still believed in Santa, so I easily believed in monsters, ghouls and goblins. It didn't help that my dad always joked saying that if he shaved my head you would find 666 on it; maybe I was a little devil after all!!

As for pumpkins, well, that's a whole other story. I never had a pumpkin as a child, doesn't matter how much I asked for a pumpkin to carve, I never got one. Apparently, so I'm told, pumpkins were expensive back in the 'old' days so all I ever got was a bloody Swede. And I don't mean a twenty one year old blonde girl with pony tails!! Each year, I was handed a Swede, a small brown and purple vegetable, also known as a turnip in some parts of the world. It would be carved, cut, and sitting on our tiled kitchen window ledge all within the space of ten minutes. I think this is what broke me and still haunts me to this day. However I can't complain, my parents always looked after me and spoilt me rotten, they still do! And by now I have learnt to appreciate the magical quality of the humble Swede!

It was when I moved out and had my own place that I could play with Halloween, and of course have my very own pumpkins to carve. Just before I got married I had a small flat, and there were two things I couldn't wait for – one was my new TV, and the other was Halloween. This is where my passion for Halloween took over, each year more decorations, more lighting and more props; it's now come to the point where my wife has to actually physically stop me from buying Halloween decorations. It's amazing the odd looks you get as a husband and wife wrestle each other over what Halloween decoration's go into shopping trolley!

After working in the games and movie memorabilia industry I wanted my own business, I was getting tired of being told what to do, and no matter what target I hit, it just got raised the following month. Don't get me wrong, I loved some of the things I did, but I don't like being told what to do, so time to become self-employed.

In 2006 I created Fright Factory UK and the amount of interest was out of this world, with many people wanting to get involved and know more. In 2007, just after my trip to Halloween Horror Nights in Florida, I was diagnosed with testicular cancer. The idea of the trip to Florida was to come back with more ideas and ways of forwarding the Fright Factory UK project. This sadly had to be put on hold so I could have the cancer removed straight away. My treatment and chemotherapy was short and I'd like to think I didn't go on about it. However I had to be positive, I even joked about it, but that's how I handled the negativity of it all I guess. My family and friends were incredible at this time, and that support owes a lot to my recovery. Now I have the all clear and can concentrate on moving forward with new and exciting ideas, this being one of them.

So here I am, writing a book all about my favourite holiday, and what an honour it is co-authoring with Mr. Hughes. The experience has been a pleasure, well most of the time; there are days when we could kill each other! But I guess that is in keeping with the season!

I live with my wife and daughter in the West Midlands.

Happy Halloween folks!

Kristoffer Hughes

A black bin bag and a Swede – I hold those two items entirely responsible for my fanatical, verging on the obsessive and somewhat crazy love of the Halloween season. In fact I would go as far as to say that it's all my Mother's fault, sorry Mum! Apparently we couldn't afford a Pumpkin, surely they weren't that expensive! So, the humble Swede was the only alternative in 1970's Wales! Don't get me wrong, I have nothing against Swede, in fact it is a lovely vegetable and works really well when mashed with good potato, but have you ever tried hollowing one out as a 7 year old child? Believe me; the joints of my right hand are permanently damaged by my efforts to disembowel a Swede! After what felt like hours of endless carving the final result was...well...pathetic to be honest, hardly worth the effort for a tiny 6 inch diameter root vegetable that hardly resembled the glorious, orange, glowing Pumpkins of the kids next door. Oh and do observe that I said Pumpkins, in the pleural, yep you got it, they had several, enormous, magnificent Pumpkins, and little Kris had to make do not only with a Swede but with a freaking bin bag as a cloak!

Of course my opinion of the humble Swede has changed significantly since, and they are now firmly rooted in my own personal Halloween traditions, but as a child I loathed and despised the things.

Consequently, by proxy of bin-bag and Swedes, I was traumatised, scarred for life and no doubt; as you may perceive from the words above, just a little bitter and perhaps a smidge twisted as a result. But every cloud has a silver lining we are told, alas my clouds remained tumultuous, black, lightning ridden clouds that would crash overhead in bitterness of those who had magnificent Pumpkins! I would grow into adulthood with the slightly unhealthy attitude of "I will not be outdone or have to carve another bloody Swede again!" Hmmm in hindsight (such a marvellous thing), I thank my Mother for the humble Swede and the familiar sound only a bin bag can make when its tied around a child's neck like some cheap garrotting device. Without that trauma I may have turned my back on Halloween.

Instead it has become a genuine obsession, bordering on the mad, yes I admit, but harmlessly fabulous at the same time; although I doubt my bank balance would agree! With a loft full to the brim of every form of Halloween decoration one could imagine. Yes, that does include a full size coffin! A November credit card statement that can cause the blood to run cold, I can safely say that I have indeed become the local "Scream Queen" the reigning champion of Halloween. A title I must admit I hold with some pride!

I live a somewhat extraordinary life, I have a peculiar job working as a Technologist in Mortuaries (Morgue for our American cousins), and I am also a writer. I see terrible things in my professional life and yet go to pieces and scream like a girl when met with a plastic mask and a bit of nylon webbing! What is that all about! I love to be scared out of my wits, to feel my bowels loosening at the sight of a cheap zombie or a sharp shock in a haunted attraction.

Amidst the fear that we feel and the exaggerated sense of terror, it still feels safe, we are permitted to scream, to run in fear of a masked man with a chainsaw prop. Perhaps it unleashes something within us that is older and primal. We are no longer hunted by man eating predators (well at least not in the United Kingdom), but we are subjected to other forms of threat, terrorism, crime, natural disasters. Halloween and its associated, fake terror permits us to express fear in a healthy manner, to scream and fall to the knees in utter terror and to then laugh about it. It's safe, yet feels totally unsafe at the time. Maybe that's why so many of us like it.

As a man quickly approaching his forties, Halloween has become a fixed part of my life; it is almost always in my thoughts, preparing, purchasing, and planning. But above all it is special, I value the time spent with the people I love, to remember loved ones who have died. I adore the celebration of it, the tackiness and fun-terror-filled nights, the familiar cries of "Trick-or-Treat" from delighted little ghouls with themed baskets and bags. Above all, there is a magical quality to the Halloween festivities that go beyond the trauma of Swedes and the fortune I spend on decorations, there is something hiding behind it all that compels me. I can think of no better words than "I just love it".

I met Mark Doody a few years ago now, and somehow there was a link, we share a common obsession, yet in many ways we are completely different. I am the screamer in the partnership, he is the sensible one, the one who doesn't crash to the floor like a wet, screaming cloth, yet secretly loves to be scared witless. My background is different from Mark's; I come from a Celtic family with Welsh being my Mother-tongue, my practise of the festival combine's aspects of Samhain and Halloween, the sublime and the profane. Mark's influence comes from the silver screen, mine from a mixture of Celticism and the movies, we hope that that unique combination has provided you the reader with a new, fresh look at Halloween. Apart we are individual obsessives; together we are a Halloween force to be reckoned with!

I live on the island of Anglesey; off the coast of North Wales.

To contact the authors please email
HalloweenHQ@hotmail.co.uk

RESOURCES

Many people and organisations have been invaluable in the creation of this book, and others have served to inspire us, these are listed here.

Midnight Syndicate – Producers of music renowned for its gothic, sinister, Halloween quality. Frequently used at haunted attractions and theme parks. Midnight Syndicate are a must for anyone wanting a suitable sinister atmosphere at their Halloween event.

Find them at www.midnightsyndicate.com

Kate and Corwen – Two of Britain's finest collectors, recorders and performers of traditional folk music. Their extensive website is full of information and all the songs can be listened to. Follow the link below and click 'Miscellaneous' to hear a rendition of a traditional Cheshire Soul Cake Song.

www.ancientmusic.co.uk/sounds.html

Halloweeneriffic - This UK based website if full of valuable information, tips, ideas, products reviews, recipes and a hoard of other useful titbits. Halloweenerrific is created by another fastidious fan of Halloween providing the Brits with reviews, and invaluable information. The site can be found at:

www.halloweeneriffic.co.uk

Hobbycraft – is Britain's largest craft and hobby store, with masses of products for all year round use, but particularly useful for

Halloween related crafting products. They have stores nationwide and also sell their good online. Find them at –

www.hobbycraft.co.uk

Wendy Andrew – Wendy's enigmatic paintings are an inspiration particularly her Samhain/Halloween themed prints and cards. Check out her beautiful website to discover one of Britain's finest independent artists.

www.paintingdreams.co.uk

Rubber Gorilla – Neal Harvey is the creator and force behind Rubber Gorilla, a British based company who make the most incredible and terrifying latex masks, available in half face or full head styles. The range is incredible and each item is individually and terrifyingly hand crafted. No Halloween costume would be the same without a Rubber Gorilla mask!

www.rubbergorilla.co.uk

Party Delights – this British based online store is one of the UK's most comprehensive one stop shops for Halloween products. Their prices are competitive, and they deliver quickly and efficiently. And unlike a lot of websites you can call them and speak to a real human being on the other side of the phone. They can be found at this address:

www.partydelights.co.uk

Woolworths – What used to be a British institution sadly closed their doors in 2009, Woolworths were the shops where you could literally buy anything, and were often the heart of a towns shopping area. However, they now have an online store and their Halloween range is even better than it used to be in store. With original products and great costumes for kids and adults alike, they continue to provide excellent seasonal goodies for the discerning buyer. Find them at:

www.woolworths.co.uk/halloween

Horror Clinic – This European based store dedicated to all things Halloween and gory has an incredible website with tons of wonderful products that you will just have to buy! Although not based in the UK the authors consider them worthy of listing as a valued resource. Their prices are quoted in British pounds and Euros and their delivery to the UK is quick and efficient. Check them out at:

www.horrorclinic.com

Spirit Halloween – This has got to be the best, the biggest and contain the widest range of Halloween paraphernalia on the planet! However the bad news is, they are based in the United States of America and alas do not deliver to the United Kingdom! But, their website is worth a look and if, like the authors, you are fortunate to visit the USA during October, you may want to consider coming home by ship to avoid excess airline baggage charges! Their website address is:

www.spirithalloween.com

The Laughing Stock – another firm favourites with the authors, this online store is packed full of Halloween goodies, some of them equalling products available in the United States. Their delivery is quick with excellent customer service, competitive prices and their website is easy to navigate. Find them at:

www.thelaughingstock.co.uk

Party Box – another online store of spooky goodies from large props to table wear. They also provide a personalised banner service to add a unique touch to your home haunt. Find them here:

www.partybox.co.uk

British Supermarkets – In recent years more and more supermarkets have invested in the massive increase of Halloween's popularity. In 2010 all the major supermarkets were crammed with original Halloween products. ASDA supermarkets were purchased by the Wal-Mart group and have since vastly increased their Halloween range, causing the other main players to pursue the season with greater vigour. Some of the larger supermarkets may have upwards of two lengths of aisle shelving to display their range of products. Stiff competition ensures that prices are kept low.

The main Supermarkets with the best choice of products are ASDA, TESCO, SAINSBURY, THE COOP and MORRISONS.

Not resources in themselves, but still worthy of note are the various theme parks that provide a quintessentially Halloween atmosphere.

Alton Towers Resort – this hugely popular and thrilling theme park resort, host their annual Halloween *Scarefest* during selected dates in October. Combining excellent facilities and specialised events in a truly spooktacular setting, this is a firm Halloween favourite. Find them at

www.altontowers.com

Thorpe Park – is the ultimate horror destination for Halloween. Fright Nights return every October providing several nights of fear at the nation's Thrill Capital. Here, visitors can experience a whole different Park after dark on some of Europe's most extreme rides before braving the Park's live action horror mazes.

www.thorpepark.com

Chessington World of Adventures – host their annual *Halloween Hocus Pocus* event, during selected dates in October and offers a spooky excursion that is also child friendly.

www.chessington.com

Legoland Windsor – this popular theme park holds a child friendly Halloween event with spectacular fireworks. Selected dates in October;

www.legoland.co.uk

Gullivers – another excellent theme park built with kids in mind, they host a child friendly Halloween event with fireworks during October.

www.gulliversfun.co.uk

Tulleys Farm – this West Sussex based farm host one of Britain's most successful Halloween events, and were voted the UK's number 1 attraction in 2008 by the *Screamie Awards*. Their *Shocktober Fest Scream Park* runs during selected dates in October. The event is held on a third generation family run farm, and is Britain's most successful independent Halloween production. For further information find them here:

www.halloweenattractions.co.uk

Although the following attractions are further afield they are worthy of mention and each provide an interactive, intensely spectacular Halloween event.

Universal Orlando Resort, Florida – the ever popular *Halloween Horror Nights* is a firm hit with British visitors to the entertainment capital of the world. Held during selected dates during

September and October, they have become experts at scaring the life out of their guests with a dizzying array of attractions and superb rides. Find them at -

www.universalorlando.com

www.halloweenhorrornights.com

Busch Gardens Tampa Bay, Florida – another hit with the British tourist, this beautiful park in Tampa is transformed into the nightmarish world of Howl O Scream during dates in September and October. With intense, terrifying walk through haunted houses and attractions and impressive rides, this event is worth a visit. Find them at –

www.buschgardens.com   www.howloscream.com

Walt Disney World Resort – Orlando, Florida – possibly the most quintessential theme park in the world, and hardly in need of introduction. However, the Walt Disney World park host their "*Mickey's not so scary Halloween Party*" during select dates in September, October and November, and is ideally suited for children. Find them at

www.disneyworld.disney.go.com

Europa Park, Germany – this park has won numerous awards and is without a doubt the most comprehensive, intense Halloween event in Europe. The award-winning park is transformed into a living nightmare as *Terenzi Horror Nights* grip its guests. Find them at –

www.terenzihorrornights.com

Port Aventura, Spain – host an annual Halloween event that lasts almost 2 months in duration! Set in a sunny, warm climate and popular with visitors from all over Europe, this park is transformed into a spooky Halloween kingdom, filled with attractions and mazes. Find them at –

www.portaventura.co.uk

BIBLIOGRAPHY

Campbell, Joseph. *The Masks of God, Primitive Mythology.* Viking Press, New York. 1959.

Cullum, Elizabeth. *A Cottage Herbal.* David & Charles, London. 1975.

Cunliffe, Barry. *The Ancient Celts.* Oxford University Press, Oxford. 1997.

Day, Brian. *Chronicles of Celtic Folk Customs.* Hamlyn, London. 2000.

De Ville, Morgana (ed). *Halloween Celebrations.* Southwater, London. 2007.

Dunwich, Gerina. *A Witch's Halloween.* Adams Media, Massachusetts. 2007.

Eason, Cassandra. *Ancient Wisdom.* Parragon, Bath. 1999.

Green, Miranda J. *Exploring the World of the Druids.* Thames and Hudson, London. 1997.

Gordon, Alice (ed) for Martha Stewart Living Omnimedia inc. *Halloween: The Best of Martha Stewart Living.* Clarkson Potter, New York. 2001.

Heimann, Jim (ed). *Halloween: Vintage Holiday Graphics*. Taschen, London. 2005.

Hole, Christina. *A Dictionary of British Folk Customs*. Granada, London. 1979.

Hutton, Ronald. *The Pagan Religions of the Ancient British Isles*. BCA, London. 1991.

Hutton, Ronald. *The Stations of the Sun, a History of the Ritual Year in Britain*. Oxford University Press, Oxford. 1996.

Isaac, Evan. *Coelion Cymru*. Y Clwb Llyfrau Cymreig, Aberystwyth. 1938.

Jones, Gordon (ed). *Celebrating a Celtic Halloween*. Gwasg Carreg Gwalch, Llanrwst. 2005.

Mabey, Richard. *Food for free*. Collins, London. 1972.

Markale, Jean. *The Pagan Mysteries of Halloween*. Inner Traditions, Vermont. 2001.

Oxbrow, Mark. *Halloween: Pagan Festival to Trick or Treat*. Strega, Guildford. 2001.

Pryor, Francis. *Britain B.C.* Harper Collins, London. 2003.

Ravenwolf, Silver. *Halloween: Customs, Recipes & Spells*. Llewellyn, St.Paul. 2002.

Rogers, Nicholas. *Halloween: From Pagan Ritual to Party Night*. Oxford University Press, Oxford. 2002.

Ross, Anne. Druids, *Preachers of Immortality*. Tempus, Stroud. 1999.

Tilley, Sophie Jane & Welby, Susan. *The Doughcraft Sourcebook*. Chancellor Press, London. 1995

Woman's Day. *A Ghostly Good Time*. Filipacchi, New York. 2008.

DISCLAIMER
or
Next time "Use Your Common Sense!"

Whilst every sensibility and caution were utilised in the making of all decorations, foods, drinks and games that appear in this book. The authors cannot be held responsible if, in your Halloween wisdom, you decide to add 5 litres of Vodka to a drink recipe, dress like a caveman and do a jack knife onto Regent Street from a hotel rooftop!

Folk don't need to be patronised when it comes to safety, but just use your common sense, keep the kids safe and make sure they know YOUR drill during YOUR Halloween outing or event.

We created this book so that others can share in our love of Halloween, but like all human beings we are flawed, so please don't hold us responsible if you accidently gas yourself in the oven whilst making Salt Dough decorations. And if you do slice your hand off cutting a lime for *Slaughtered on the Beach*, become septic or suffer any other tomfoolery, and subsequently die, hey-ho, we guess it's ultimately good for the gene-pool, and we'll see you on the other side.

Thank you for buying our book, Toodle-Pip!

> *At first Cock-Crow,*
> *The ghosts must go,*
> *Back to their quiet graves below.*
> *(Theodosia Garrison 1874 – 1944)*

Index

NATURAL DRUIDRY
by Kristoffer Hughes

Natural Druidry is a deeply personal account of one man's journey through the dappled groves of culture and tradition. Exploring the inspiration of Druidry through the eyes of a man in love with heritage and the land, Kris takes you on a journey into the mysteries of the Druid tradition, into the shadows of the past and the magic of Druidry.

Written with simplistic clarity, humour and tears, Kris invites you to share his journey through tradition, descending into the mysteries of Druidry and of its practise in the twenty-first century. Exploring the fundamental principles of Druidry from ritual, connection, mythology, shamanism and finally to a personal ride through the Druid year.

Share in a world of wondrous beings, of sheer potentiality beyond comprehension and the awe and childlike surrender one feels when confronted with the enchantment of Druidry.

Inspiration lies at the heart of this book, where the joyous experience of the flowing spirit of Druidry known as Awen sings through dry ink. Journey with Kris into the magic of the past and the present, deep into the vast cauldron of spiritual enlightenment that sings from the land, that whispers to us upon the breeze as the breath of our ancestors.

ISBN 978-1-870450-67-6

www.ingramcontent.com/pod-product-compliance
Lightning Source LLC
Chambersburg PA
CBHW051209090426
42740CB00021B/3428